Pra

In *The Alchemy of Grief,* Nancy Loeffler shares her heart-wrenching and ultimately empowering journey through the wild territory of loss. Like a true alchemist, she has transformed the nuggets of wisdom gained from her experiences into practical tools that can help anyone who's coping with grief to find their way home. This is a beautiful and heartfelt book.

—Marc David & Emily Rosen, *Institute for the Psychology of Eating*

Nancy Loeffler beautifully articulates what it means to live through significant loss, and how to live well after. *The Alchemy of Grief* provides support and guidance for the bereaved, allowing one to explore the ways in which the "what was" can be reconciled with the "what is", so to create an anchor for the "what now".

—Ryla Jules, *Community Manager @ The Dinner Party (thedinnerparty.org)*

Nancy has soul-deep experience with grief. Those courageous people ready to face their grief will discover a teacher, a mentor, and a friend to lead them through their journey with wise words, helpful activities, and constant companionship.

—Wendy S., *Client*

In *The Alchemy of Grief,* Nancy artfully weaves back and forth between her memories, rich with powerful emotion, and thoughtful, practical suggestions on processing grief. She fully demonstrates that "losing her daughter is too high a price to pay to not be herself", and illustrates beautifully the journey of self-discovery that began with her daughter's death. Whether you or someone you care about is grieving, *The Alchemy of Grief* will touch you, educate you, inspire you. I can do the work no justice in a few lines. Read it for yourself.

—Doreen Devoy-Hulgan

For the purpose of supporting and guiding others through grief, Nancy Loeffler is willing to share an intimate insight into her raw pain after the tragic death of her teenage daughter. In *The Alchemy of Grief,* she sensitively takes the reader through her painful experience and her resulting, and deliberate, growth. Nancy offers practical guidance, with specific actions, for those who are numbed and paralyzed by grief.

This book will guide those working to understand and support the process and prepare each of us for the inevitable grieving we will all experience.

—Ella Sciarra, *Bereavement Minister*

Travel with Nancy as she leads you through her journey of grief following the loss of her 17-year-old daughter Leah. She shares touching personal moments and helps you work through your own time of grieving; whatever the loss. Her insightful questions and journaling ideas allow you to examine how you can move forward at your own speed as you navigate this frightening and overwhelming time in your life. A book to read, work through and share with anyone who needs help on their grief journey.

—Alice Watrobka, *Proud to be a long-time friend*

Nancy Loeffler's book *The Alchemy of Grief* is so full of kindness and gentleness that despite the subject matter of overwhelming loss, there is great comfort and potential for immense healing. Loeffler shares her story of losing of her 17-year-old daughter Leah. By touching her own specific moments of grief, by recognizing what she was feeling both early on and in all the days that followed, seeing both the agony and the gifts, she gives the reader full permission to do the same.

This book feels like a true and loyal companion for the toughest journey you'll ever make. There's no other book I'd want to have with me than this one.

Her words feel like a massage, an excavation and unconditional love all at once. She also offers super helpful journaling questions and suggestions for self-care, self-understanding and letting go of expectations for "how to grieve" for those who are grieving. I recommend this book wholeheartedly!

—Anne Heaton, *Singer, Songwriter*

Grief is inevitable, and unfortunately because it's usually an uncomfortable topic, we are grossly underprepared to deal with it when it strikes us. This book beautifully shares the story of Nancy's personal journey with grief associated with losing her daughter, and gives readers a framework to navigate their own journey regardless of the type of loss. Having recently lost my mother, I found that this book gave me a practical framework for how to be with my grief, and gave me an actual skill set to help my grief journey become more productive and bearable. As a mother, I sometimes wonder how I would ever survive losing one of my children. This book provided a very comforting picture of what is possible when a family is willing to be with their grief, and offers support and tools for the journey. I'm deeply grateful for Nancy's courage to walk her own journey, and then share her lessons and experiences with the world in this very special book.

—Summer Deaton

"Losing her is too high a price to pay to not live the life I am meant to live."

Who are YOU meant to be?

That is the question this book will guide you to answer as it leads you down a path of healing from inextricable loss.

To know loss is to be human, which is why I say *The Alchemy of Grief* is an opportunity for anyone who seeks meaning from life, at all stages of their journey.

Not only does Nancy demonstrate a process of being with yourself, wherever you are in your journey of grief, she presents an opportunity to appreciate life, with all of its twisted turns and beautifully heart-wrenching moments.

Nancy offers tools that balance gentle, compassionate and firm love. Through her generous sharing, she helps you negotiate your desire to indulge the present moment while remaining committed to moving forward, finding meaning, and remembering that you are whole.

Nancy's true gift is in framing grief as an opportunity to live in alignment with the truth of who you are. She skillfully removes all shame from the experience and gifts you with a sense of peace and permission to be exactly where you are. This is NOT a book designed to teach you how to grieve, so much as it is a book that will invite you in to yourself, connecting you to your own knowing, and giving you permission to claim your own path.

—Dawn M. Dalili, *ND*

Experience *The Alchemy of Grief* and awaken to the many ways life changes impact our total being. By sharing her story of loss and by providing reflective prompts and exercises, Nancy Loeffler leads the reader along a path of healing and renewal.

—Rob Nerius

Despite being inundated with stress management tools and techniques, we remain buried under a collective stress that is showing up as social media diatribes, illness, relational conflicts, and the downward spiral of numbing addictions. I suspect the culprit is not modern life, as some would say, but rather our unmetabolized grief. We fear the great lions of sadness and loss, yet fully embodying them - and the love that allows them - is what Nancy Loeffler, in her new book *The Alchemy of Grief*, is suggesting. Based on her heartbreaking experience of losing a child, she compassionately guides us along the healing pathway that courage and grace walked her through. Significant is not only relying on this for times of major transition (which it excels at), but also to accompany us through small and everyday woes and sorrows. By developing a practice to slalom through the quotidian gates of loss, we are prepared to withstand the storms. Resilience is what this book teaches - how to live with the vicissitudes of our own and others' journeys. What Elizabeth Kubler Ross did for the stages of dying, Loeffler is doing for the stages of coming back to the living.

—Kellie Brooks, *Founder and Lead Trainer, The Hospitality Edge*

The Alchemy of Grief is a beautifully written, compelling expression of what it means to suffer and ultimately make peace with a life-shattering loss. With wisdom and eloquence, Ms. Loeffler explores the many layers and dimensions of grief as a life-long journey of healing and transformation. She carries the reader through the many phases of loss and grief, offering personal insight, practical advice and self-care strategies. Intelligent and compelling, this book is a true gift to anyone suffering the pain of loss and grief.

—Cheryl C., *LCPC, and grief survivor*

The Alchemy of Grief is a beautifully written, compelling expression of what it means to suffer and ultimately make peace with a life-shattering loss. With wisdom and eloquence, Ms. Loeffler explores the many layers and dimensions of grief as a lifelong journey of healing and transformation. She carries the reader through the many phases of loss and grief, offering personal insight, practical advice, and self-care strategies. Intelligent and compelling, this book is a true gift to anyone suffering the pain of loss and grief.

The Alchemy of Grief is so much more than the story of a mother's tragic loss. It is also a VERY readable, simple examination of the various stages, levels, and types of grief that one encounters throughout life. Along with the touching story, Nancy Loeffler provides reflective questions and activity examples that serve as a map for almost limitless grief healing pathways. The book, which can be referenced time and again, is suitable for any individual's personality and needs. Personally, the last chapter really "spoke to my heart," and as a whole, I feel that this wonderful book should be on everyone's bookshelf.

—Mary McNaughton

You are such a Blessing to those grieving, who have a difficult journey ahead of them, by letting them know they can find more Love, Grace, and Peace in the process, by understanding, and exploring their hearts and emotions further. Your book, *The Alchemy of Grief*, will profoundly touch the lives of many who need to hear your heartfelt message, in knowing they can heal and feel whole inside again, especially when there is self-doubt, guilt, anger, or denial present after such a devastating loss. You've traveled a road less traveled that wasn't easy, and did it with such loving awareness, reflection, fierceness, compassion, and understanding!

I loved how your notes at the end of each chapter allowed for further reflection, check-ins, guidance, encouragement, and practical steps to help overcome and integrate the grieving process into one's life daily, monthly, yearly. This is so critical to rebuilding lives, and creating new traditions around milestones reached that honor the remembrance of the person who has passed. I loved that you shared how emotions can be expressed naturally in a healthy, beautiful way, empowering the person who is grieving. This gives new meaning to living our Life to the fullest in each moment, and being present and grateful for our Life. Perhaps, as mentioned, these are some of the greatest gifts we can receive in moving through this soul-filled grieving process.

— Dr. Jan Lei Iwata, *DO, PharmD, MS*
www.drjanleiiwata.com

The Alchemy of Grief:

Your Journey to Wholeness

Foreword by
Sheila A. Foster, MA

NANCY LOEFFLER

First Printing, 2016

ISBN 978-0-9978330-0-3

1. Spirituality 2. Self Help 3. New Age 4. Metaphysical

Ordering Information: Special discounts are available on quantity purchases by corporations, associations, and others. For details, contact the author.

www.beingwithgrief.com

Published by Brand & Book, an imprint of Cynergie Studio.

Raleigh, North Carolina | www.brandandbook.com

Author photo: Lori Nagel, Sunflower Studios

Writing coach: Max Regan

Book design: Cyn Macgregor

Set in Adobe Garamond and Autour One

Printed in the United States of America

The Alchemy of Grief:
Your Journey to Wholeness

Nancy Loeffler

With a foreword by Sheila A. Foster

www.beingwithgrief.com

Brand & Book
empowering authors

An imprint of Cynergie Studio
BRANDANDBOOK.COM

Dedication

This book is dedicated with Love to

Leah Therese Loeffler,

for shining your light into our lives

and

Dan and Peter Loeffler

There is no one else I would rather travel with on this journey

Acknowledgments

So many people have helped bring this book into the world, whether they know it or not.

To Max Regan, your brilliance helped me to bring form and structure to my wild ramblings and made me believe that I am a writer.

To Sheila Foster, for your heartfelt foreword, your words bring tears of recognition to my eyes. Thank you for showing me how to follow the breadcrumbs in the unknown as well as the way to my own heart.

To the entire community of the Temple of the Sacred Feminine, I began this initiation with you many moons ago and I have continued to invoke your presence throughout my journey whenever I needed to be uplifted.

To Dena, for walking with me on this rocky road and for always being a beacon in the darkness.

To our family and friends, every single one of you, you supported us through the devastating loss of our beloved Leah. You cared for us with prayers, love, food, and so much more. There's not a doubt in my mind that we continue to be buoyed up by your love and prayers to this day.

To my Whiting-Turner family, you cared for us as one of your own as we learned to live with our new normal.

To Cyn Macgregor, your creativity and attention to detail brought the dream of writing my book into reality. Thank you for guiding me through a process that was unknown to me with so much fun and humor.

To Miranda Volborth, your editing of my words brought clarity to my story.

To Dawn and Ali for asking the right questions at the right time, and to my entire Priestess Mistressmind Group, for holding space, midwifing, and witnessing the birth of my true work in the world.

To Ella, Alice, Rob, Mary, Marc, Emily, Dawn, Kellie, Anne, Summer, Jan, Doreen, Cheryl, Wendy, and Ryla for reading my manuscript and providing your feedback. This work is better because of your kind words.

To all of my amazing clients, you have taught me more than you know.

To Peter and AlyssA, for constant love, encouragement, and support.

To Dan, my beloved, you were the first to recognize my true essence.
There are no words to describe your faithful love and unfailing support as we
traveled on our path all these years.

To Leah, I wouldn't have missed it for the world.

Leah Therese Loeffler

Foreword

It touches my heart deeply to have the honor of welcoming you into Nancy Loeffler's inspiring book, *The Alchemy of Grief: Your Journey to Wholeness*. I offer this introduction as a psychotherapist who has worked with the grief of others for nearly 40 years, and as a woman who has had many losses since birth—the most devastating being the loss of my beloved daughter, Priya, nearly 20 years ago. Grief is no stranger to any of us; it is part of every human life. It is the raw, excruciating, shadow side of loving. We grieve the loss of people we love as well as so many other things in our lives when someone precious to us is no longer physically here. It's as if a tornado has swept through and shattered what we knew our lives and ourselves to be, and we are left stunned, broken, on our knees in the chaos. Then, when reality hits, the grief begins...

I met Nancy in 2001, when she entered the Temple of the Sacred Feminine, a contemporary women's mystery school that I founded in 1987. This was nearly a year after her seventeen-year-old daughter, Leah, lost her life in a car accident and Nancy was still deep in her grieving process. The Temple is a safe, sacred space where Nancy was held in loving community with other women and where she learned practices and processes for healing trauma and heartbreak, for awakening spiritually, and for cultivating skills as a healing practitioner. Central to all that the Temple offers is the inner yoga of Samyama, an extraordinary heart-opening practice that was, and is, central to Nancy's grief journey and her life. In 2005, Nancy participated in the first two-year training I offered in Samyama Healing and is now a highly skilled certified Samyama Practitioner as well as grief counselor. As you will see throughout her book, Samyama heart practice gave her a way to embrace her grief and be able to meet the most difficult moments by going to her heart.

The Alchemy of Grief: Your Journey to Wholeness is a guide for anyone who is feeling their grief or for those who are ready to take down the walls around old grief and release it. Grief is alchemy: it offers a profound change of heart that allows us to continue to love our lost beloved without feeling a sense of betraying them, and to go on to have a rich and fulfilling life in honor of them. Through grief work, we discover that though the tender wound of grief in our hearts remains, and is touched from time to time, it no longer overwhelms or consumes our lives. Nancy begins her story with a compelling account of the shocking news from the police that her daughter, Leah, was in a car accident on her way to school. Her very vulnerable writing immediately takes you into the surreal sense of being in "a foreign country," as she names it. We see what she sees, and hear her conversations with others, as well as those within her own mind. Because Nancy is so aware of her feelings, it is possible to feel what she feels as we read. *The Alchemy of Grief: Your Journey to Wholeness* is the heart-opening and heart-rending story of Nancy's courage, willingness, and fierce commitment to open her own heart fully to feel her immeasurable grief, to meet and embrace every raw and painful moment as it appeared, to receive the teachings of the moment, and to realize the gifts (yes, gifts!) as they appeared. She shares writings from her journal, offers her own self-inquiry, and speaks of how important it was to take care of herself by committing a certain time daily to sit with her feelings. Nancy offers the raw, real, pure, wide, and wild array of emotions and behaviors that grief can bring forth. She tells us what it was like living in her grief, in the midst of daily life; she touches on ordinary things such as work, dealing with people who had no idea what to say or how to be with her, and the renovation of her family's house—an out-picturing of the destruction and re-building of their lives after Leah's death. I especially love the many profound insights that she weaves throughout the book that come to her by way of tending her own heart, witnessing her own feelings and behavior, keeping a journal, and engaging in self-inquiry. An especially provocative message that she received as a whole-body knowing the day after Leah's death was, "Everything you have done up until this point has prepared you for what is next." Think about that.

Nancy also shares the numerous synchronicities and magical moments that she still experiences as communications from Leah. This is very common if we are open to this possibility. Those we love, whose physical presence is no longer here, are still with us in their soul presence; we can love them and sometimes feel their company even if we can no longer have their physical presence. I found the "Things to Try" and "Questions for Your Journal" that were at the end of each chapter replete with excellent practical ways to help resource resilience and heart healing. These inquiries and suggestions invite you into the inner work that served Nancy's healing and resilience, and they can make a huge difference if you are grieving, and you take them on when you are ready. The last chapter of the book offers support and practical suggestions for people who are supporting someone else who is grieving the deep loss of a loved one.

The Alchemy of Grief: Your Journey to Wholeness is filled with so many poignant moments that tears welled up many times. Here is one exquisite example that Nancy shares about their visit to the hospital while Leah was still on life support:

Dan and I began to walk down the stairs of the parking garage. At the landing I heard the chirps of a scared little sparrow that was trying to find its way out of the stairwell. Dan walked over to the frightened bird.

"Here you go, little sparrow, let me help you find your way out," he said. I watched him shepherd the bird to an open window. "It's ok, you can fly free now," Dan said. The bird flew away, warbling its thanks.

This touched me because it reminded me that we are held by Divine Arrangement and we can trust that what is needed is given at the perfect time. As human beings living life in the midst of impermanence, imperfection, and incompletion, we all lose people we love and we all experience grief, but we don't necessarily know how to be with it, feel it, or be with others who are deeply grieving. Nancy has an extraordinarily intimate understanding of the grief process, self-care during grief, and how to relate to others who may not know how to relate to you in your grief. She is offering a beautiful, healthy model for a grief journey that is much needed by many who lack resources in this area.

In honoring and trusting her own grief to lead the way, transformation happened for Nancy, and she has been able to rise from the ashes of her old life to emerge into a new life that honors her daughter. With Leah's ongoing inspiration, Nancy's fulfilling new life has an exquisitely beautiful new purpose—that of walking with others on their own grief journeys through the diverse landscapes of their shattered hearts. This new life is shared with her husband, Dan, who, through his own grief journey, trained to became a grief counselor. Throughout the book, Nancy speaks of Leah as her teacher and acknowledges the many ways Leah's loving presence is still with her, and still teaching her—and now teaching those of us who read this beautifully written book. If you are currently grieving, if you have shut down your grief, or if you are supporting someone who is grieving, reading and receiving the offerings of *The Alchemy of Grief: Your Journey to Wholeness* can touch your heart, transmute your grief, and help restore a sense of wholeness to you and your life.

Sheila A. Foster, MA
Transpersonal Psychotherapist
Initiatory Elder and Founder, Temple of the Sacred Feminine
Boulder, CO
www.templeofthesacredfeminine.com
www.facebook.com/templeofthesacredfeminine

Contents

Prologue

It was a Friday morning in early November. I arrived at work early that day hoping to leave a little early. Leah, my daughter, was preparing to take the SAT the next morning, and I wanted to help her settle in that night so she would be well rested in the morning. I sat down at my desk and smiled. The night before, we had sat in the living room together. She had been anxious about the upcoming test, and excited to be going with a friend to homecoming afterward. She'd had her hair done in a new way, and had asked me how I liked it. She'd looked as beautiful as always, sitting across from me. We had talked about how nervous she was to take the test, and how excited she was to be finishing high school and applying to colleges. After we had talked a little more, she'd hugged me and went to her room.

My phone rang, interrupting my musings. It was Leah.

"Hi, mom." She sounded tired. "I'm running late. Can you call school and let them know?"

I hid my exasperation. "Of course I will. Are you ok?"

"Yeah, I just woke up late."

"Ok, I'll call. Be careful."

"Thanks."

"Bye, I love you."

"Love you, too."

I called school to let them know she was running late. My exasperation returned. Not getting to school on time was a common theme. I was working with her to help her be more organized and relaxed, so she could get enough sleep and get to school on time. She wavered between self-sufficiency and reliance on our help. I wanted to help her trust her own skills as she prepared for college.

I turned my attention back to my work, looking at my lists of tasks for that day. Some time later I was interrupted by a knock on my office door. I shared my office with a co-worker, and the door is never closed, so I found this to be strange. Most people just came in and started talking to me. As I turned, I saw two campus police officers.

"Are you Nancy Loeffler?"

"Yes," I said, as fear began to creep up my spine.

"Do you have a daughter named Leah?"

"Yes…"

"Please come with us, ma'am."

"Why? What's happened? I just spoke with her."

"Please come with us, ma'am."

They took me by the elbow and led me out of the trailer, down the street, and into a waiting squad car.

"What happened? Where are you taking me?" I felt panic rising.

"There's been an accident. That's all we can tell you. We'll take you to the Frederick County Line, and the Frederick Police will take you to the hospital from there."

I called Dan and told him, as best I could, what happened. He said he would meet me at the county line.

My thoughts were all over the place. *What were you up to? Can't I trust you to go to school without getting into trouble? Who were you with? Why aren't they telling me anything? What about my car? How will it get home? I can't believe they expect me to just go with them without telling me any more than they did!*

As these thoughts came, I was furious. I didn't want to face whatever had happened. I didn't want people to think I was a bad mother who couldn't even figure out a way to help her daughter make her way in the world.

You're taking me away from my job, again… how am I going to keep this job if I always have to tend to your antics?"

Fear coursed through my body. *What am I going to find out about you that I don't want to know?*

We were driving on the expressway toward Frederick, Maryland, where we lived at the time. We pulled off on the shoulder, where another police car was waiting for us. Dan's car was there, too. Two officers got out of the police car. One got into Dan's car and the other came to escort me from the car I was in, to his car.

"What is happening?" I asked.

"The Frederick County police officers will take you from here. Your husband can follow you there."

I got into the next police car.

"What is happening? Where are we going?" I wanted to scream, but the words barely make it out of my mouth. I wondered why I couldn't drive with Dan.

"There's been an accident. We are going to the hospital."

"What happened?"

"That's all I can tell you, ma'am."

My thoughts were randomly screaming and careening around in my head. I couldn't believe that no one would tell me what happened; didn't I have a right to know? But I didn't want to know. I wanted to go back to the way things were last night.

I hear him whisper into his radio, "I have a female Caucasian, mid 40s." A pause. "Negative."

NEGATIVE WHAT, my head shrieked.

We sat in silence for the duration of the ride. I asked a couple more questions, but I got no answers. The ride took forever, even though I knew he was going faster than the speed limit. What was Dan thinking, in the car behind us? We hadn't had a chance to talk. I wondered if they had told him any more than they had told me.

I didn't know it at the time—I certainly didn't know it on that day— but the loss of somebody that you love, and living with that loss, is exactly like crossing the border to a new, unfamiliar country. The language is nebulous and the ground unrecognizable. My grief journey was an invitation to live in a new country, one to which I had never wanted to move. The land I left behind is different than the land that I was forced to enter. On that day, as I was transported to the hospital, I crossed from one county to another. I didn't know I was living a metaphor; it was just a day unfolding like any other. You may be in the midst of crossing that border right now. If you are, I hope this book will be useful to you as you become acquainted with your new landscape.

One of the best ways to use this book is to buy a journal, and to let it keep you company as you read. At the end of each chapter there will be a list of things to try and questions for you to answer. Your journal is a place where you can record your thoughts and track your progress. It can be your companion on your own unique journey.

—Nancy Loeffler, June 13, 2016

Sometimes I am still back on Nov. 2nd sitting in our living room,
talking to Leah, the day before the accident...
I want that day back.
I want to hold her in my arms and not let her out of my sight.
I want to keep her here for all of us.

—From My Journal, 8/18/2001

CHAPTER 1
You're Never Prepared

A New Reality

When a catastrophic event happens, your life changes in an instant. It may take some time for you to arrive to your new reality. Your life can take on a surreal quality. You may be in shock; you may feel like you are living in a haze, where everything around you seems distorted. You may be unable to concentrate on anything; everything may be hyper clear, or moving in slow motion. Your thoughts may explode in a million directions. There is a fracture in your life. You don't know how you are going to fix the fracture. You want to fix it, and you remember, yet again, that nothing will ever be the same. It is the space between the way things were yesterday and the land you are forced to move to, without wanting to move there. The suddenness of this fracture may mean that it will take some time for you to catch up with all the changes, both energetically and physically.

The space between the land you used to live in and the one to which you are moving can be hard to inhabit. It can be a rocky road that literally knocks you off your feet. When you take the first step across the border, you are likely to be confused, disorganized, or disoriented. I remember that I felt spacey for the first time in my life when I stepped into this place. Be gentle with yourself wherever you find yourself. All of these qualities can be characteristics of shock, and the land in between realities can serve as a protection for you. It can be a way of shielding you from the harshest reality that you now find yourself inhabiting. At the time the splintering of your life occurs, you may not be prepared for everything you will encounter. I know I wasn't. It has been only with courage, love, and support that I was able to traverse the territory in between my life before Leah died, and the inevitable life without her physical presence that followed. I was able to emerge with the ability to live a meaningful life again, and to come to know my soul in a way that would have been impossible under any other circumstances. Your own passage through grief and loss offers the same possibilities.

Entering a New Country

When I finally arrived at the hospital, it was the first time that I saw Dan that day. We hugged, holding on for dear life and hoping that when we let go, we would be back at home, waking up from a bad dream. I asked him if he knew what happened, but he didn't know any more than I did. Leah's guidance counselor and principal were there to meet us in the waiting room. They both had grim looks on their faces, and we began to gather information about what happened as we were obliviously beginning our Friday. Leah was in an accident on her way to school. She hit a tree—the only tree in the middle of a cornfield. She was alone in the car. She called 911. She had massive brain injuries and had gone into surgery. They told us she was a fighter. She was fighting for her life.

In that one moment my world was tipped on end. I felt like I was in an altered reality. It did feel like I was in a different country, one that I had never even heard of before. Everything changed from being all about me to being all about Leah. I was a mother wanting nothing more than to protect her child, her baby. Nothing else mattered—not my job, not what anyone else thought about me, not my failure as a mother. I told myself, "Once we get her through this I'm going to be the mother she needs me to be." But I couldn't stop shaking. We were taken to the critical care waiting room. I couldn't sit still. I paced back and forth, praying for my daughter's life. We called Peter, our son at college. He made plans to join us. Somehow I knew in my bones the magnitude of what we were experiencing, and after an agonizingly long wait, our lives changed forever.

Looking back on this scene from my vantage point today, I understand that the thoughts I had when the police office came into my office and told me about the accident, were normal. If that had not been the day of my daughter's accident—if she were not fighting for her life—thoughts of what she had been doing, concern for my job, and thoughts of how to help her would have been countless threads in the fabric of a normal mother-daughter relationship. At the time I felt guilty and full of shame. I ran all the "if-onlys" and "what-ifs" through my head. If only I had been home with her that morning, if only I had talked to her longer that morning, if only... I could have prevented her from having the accident, of fighting for her life.

As we live our lives, raising children, helping them learn to make good decisions as teenagers, there will be many moments of doubt and confusion. We will question our children and ourselves. We will have these same normal, universal thoughts that I had when I learned of Leah's accident. We want to control our lives and everything that happens in them, and we learn that there is really nothing in our control. We learn to trust and to have faith. At the time of my daughter's accident I was at a point in my own journey of learning to trust my intuition. I was learning how my intuition helped me to be a better mother. As I waited at the hospital, I felt that I had failed. I hadn't learned these lessons in time to keep her safe.

Dan's Perspective

My husband Dan shared a lot of similarities with me in his experience of Leah's accident, but he also felt a lot of differences. He always says that thinking back to the day of Leah's accident and thinking that she might not survive, invited him to dive again into a sea of sorrow that he floundered in for many years. When he places himself back into that time, he says that he always begins with remembering the night before.

Dan and I took turns making sure that Leah heard her alarm and was up and about. That morning when I headed out, Dan stayed behind to make sure Leah was awake and beginning her morning. Knocking on the door to her room before he left, he asked if she would be ok. He heard her say she would, so he told her goodbye, and to have a good day, and started his own morning drive. He often remembers his own "what if" moment. He wonders what would have happened if he'd insisted that she come to the door, or waited until he heard the shower running, before he left.

When Dan received my call that morning, he headed to the Frederick County Line as instructed, wondering—like me—what had happened. It took a while before Dan and I could share our thoughts about the early events of that significant day in November. We were each in our own world, feeling shock and fear within the surreal and sterile environment of the hospital. I eventually learned that he knew from the way the police handled their unpleasant task that the news would not be good; that, however, did nothing to prepare him for his first sight of Leah. The sight of her broken body hooked up to machines took him back to the last time he had sat with her, talked with her about her day, and received her last embrace the previous evening. He had hugged her and watched her bounce down the stairs as he headed out to walk the dogs. He had a smile on his face as he thought about what would be his last conversation with his daughter.

Things to Try:

When a catastrophic event happens in your life, here are some things you can do.

1. When you hear bad news, breathe. Take a few deep, slow, abdominal breaths. Tell whoever you are with to slow down and let you catch your breath.

2. If you are alone, call someone to support you.

3. Ask for what you need. If you are not getting answers that make sense, ask someone to help you get the answers, if you can. If not, stop and tell the person what you need to know. Sometimes, if we can get the information we need, it can help us to assimilate the situation and calm down a little.

4. When tragedy occurs, we can feel helpless. Acknowledging your helplessness and knowing that it is ok to accept help can be difficult. You may see it as a reflection of failure. Learning to forgive yourself and others is a part of your journey. Accept offers of assistance when offered.

5. Take time to write down your feelings, or the sequence of events. Your memory might not be as sharp as usual, and this written record can be helpful to you later on.

QUESTIONS FOR YOUR JOURNAL:

- How did you feel the moment of a sudden change in your life?
- Describe the landscape in-between the place you left and where you are headed.
- What do you need right now? This will change from day to day, or even moment to moment. Ask it often.

I drove home from work today in a driving rain
so hard I could barely see the car in front of me.
I felt Leah say, "This is how much I miss you, Mom."

—From **My Journal**, 7/22/2004

CHAPTER 2
Early Grief

Our Vigil Begins

We were camped out in the hospital waiting room. Since we had arrived here on Friday we had been keeping vigil. After Leah's surgery, her doctors told us she had a five percent chance of living through the weekend, so we stayed. The nurses prepared us to see her for the first time. They told us her head had been shaved and her face was puffy. I walked tentatively into her room, fearing I wouldn't recognize my daughter. I took a deep breath and pushed open the door. She was hooked up to so many machines I could hardly find her, and then I saw her tiny form sinking into the bed, tubes and wires running all over the place. I stopped at the door to give myself a moment to get used to how she looked, but it wasn't necessary—I recognized her. She was still beautiful, but she just looked so broken. I walked over to her side, tears beginning to stream down my face. I was relieved that I was finally seeing her, but fearful of what was ahead for us. I wondered where her spirit was. I took hold of her hand, careful not to hold it too hard or to hurt her anymore that she already was hurt. I touched her head gently. Gone was the hair she loved. I stroked her cheek. Dan and I talked to her, told her that we loved her and not to worry about the car, and asked her to come back to us. She lay there, hooked up to monitors and machines, unable to respond. She was in a medically-induced coma because of the swelling of her brain.

Friends began arriving—Leah's friends from school, and our friends from work. They met us in the waiting room when we left Leah's room for a few minutes. I wasn't sure how they knew how to find us. They arrived with food, hugs, and prayers. They supported us with their presence. They asked us for the prognosis; we didn't know what to say. Everyone believed she'd get better—how could she not? It was a nightmare more suited to a TV show or a movie than my life. Her friends gave us pictures of themselves and we hung them in her room; due to her critical nature we were the only visitors she was allowed. We told her that her friends were there, and they couldn't wait to see her and spend time with her again. Her brother, Peter, was devoted to her. He sang songs to her, reminded her of childhood memories, and made plans for the future. We grabbed on to each thin gossamer thread of hope given to us by doctors. Each time one tenuously slipped out of our grasp, we were plummeted back into the fear of the unknown. The thought of losing Leah was unimaginable to us; we couldn't even begin to comprehend her huge light missing from our lives. We continued to believe that our miracle would come.

We made it through to Monday morning. She was the same, although I thought she must've been a little better since she made it through the weekend, against all odds. That percentage had to be greater than five now, didn't it? It was the glimmer of hope that we needed. Dan and I decided to go home that night to sleep in our own bed, or at least to try. Just thinking about being able to lie down in our own bed felt like a luxury we couldn't afford ourselves just one day earlier. Peter stayed with Leah that night.

Surviving the Early Days of Grief

After a devastating loss, your feelings might be incredibly intense. They may be erratic, changeable, and unpredictable; they might feel like they are coming at you all at once. You might have days where you feel like you want to stay in bed, cover your head with your pillows, and not come out—and some days, that's the best way to take care of yourself. This stage of grief sometimes comes with an incredible emotional flow. Early grief can arrive with many physical manifestations as well as emotional ones.

What can you do when you don't feel like doing anything? When staying in bed as a distraction only makes the dreaded feelings feel even bigger? When every time you wake up from a nap, you are once again forced to remember what happened, so you avoid sleeping altogether until you are so exhausted you fall into a restless slumber that will not let you rest? There are two things that were helpful to me during this time: sleep and rest, and feeling my feelings. You may discover that pushing your feelings away only postpones their arrival.

Being with your feelings, as painful as they are, can allow them to soften. Grief in the early days can feel primitive, and the stages of grief are not linear. They can arrive in an unpredictable manner, and you may find yourself bouncing from one feeling to another, and back again. It can feel very messy and chaotic.

Finding a Way Out

Tuesday morning dawned after a fitful night's sleep. Even a restless or uneasy night's sleep in familiar surroundings went a long way to soothe our ravaged emotional state. We set out for the hospital after breakfast. We planned to let Peter come home to get some better rest, too. We drove in silence; there was nothing to say. As we approached the hospital I felt a little more hope than I did when I left there the day before. Maybe it was because I was slightly more rested. Maybe it was because she was really getting better. I allowed myself to hope that she would be able to be taken out of the coma and we would be able to talk to her. We drove into the hospital parking garage and parked the car on an upper level. Dan and I began to walk down the stairs of the parking garage. At the landing I heard the chirps of a scared little sparrow that was trying to find its way out of the stairwell. Dan walked over to the frightened bird.

"Here you go, little sparrow, let me help you find your way out," he said. I watched him shepherd the bird to an open window. "Its ok, you can fly free now," Dan said. The bird flew away, warbling its thanks.

I couldn't move. The lump in my throat was so big I could hardly breathe. My stomach was clenched, constricted with a knowing that had not yet reached my brain. That was the first moment I knew, in every cell of my body, that Leah was not coming back to us. I didn't speak this out loud. Saying it might make it true. Still, I asked for a miracle.

We arrived in her room; we hugged Peter, and listened to his report. I sat down near Leah's bed and took her hand. Tears began to flow again. Silently I said, "I love you, Leah. I want you to come back to us more than anything I have ever wanted. If you need to fly away, too, I want you to do what you need to do. I want you to be happy and free." I stroked her hand, kissed it. I kissed her head where the stubble was beginning to grow back after it was shaved a few days ago—or maybe it was a few lifetimes ago. I was not ready to say goodbye, yet somehow I did, in the best way that I could on that day.

Silently, Dan and I knew that our last vigil with Leah had begun. I spent the day looking at her beautiful, peaceful face, willing her to wake up. We didn't speak of the "sparrow incident," as we had both begun to call it. Friends continued to arrive, hers and ours. We asked permission for them to visit her in her room. All that afternoon and evening, two or three at a time, they entered her room to do something no 17- or 18-year-old should ever have to do—to say goodbye to a beloved friend. One of our friends shared his hope that his own daughter would share the same elegance that Leah showed that night.

I felt panic rising. I could go on like this indefinitely if I knew my daughter would come back to us, or even if I didn't know for sure, but had hope. How was I going to leave this place when it was time, and never go back, never see my daughter again, never hug her again, never touch her precious face, or see her light? How could I get to the next day without hearing her laugh, seeing her give me an eye roll? It was more than I could bear. I looked around at her father, her brother, her friends, our friends. I wanted to wake up from this nightmare now. I called out-of-town relatives and friends and told them it didn't look like Leah was going to get better. I heard the denial in their voices. I wanted to agree with them. Our miracle, the one we wanted to happen, was that she would open her eyes and wonder why we were all there.

Late Tuesday evening, Leah's nurse called me, Dan, and Peter into her room. We asked why, and she averted her tear-filled eyes. The doctor came in. He told us that Leah had no more brain function. "When will she regain brain function?" I asked more boldly than I felt. "She won't. She hasn't had brain activity for some time now," he said.

Our tears returned anew. We hugged each other; we didn't want to move from her room. I didn't want to leave my baby. What if we were to make the wrong decision?

"We need your consent to remove her from life support," said the nurse.

I wanted to scream. I couldn't comprehend what I had just heard. If my baby was no longer living, why did we need to give consent to take her off life support?

"We'll give you some time with your daughter to say goodbye," the nurse told us as she and the doctor left the room.

To this day I can't remember giving the consent, though we must have. The next thing I remember is going to the waiting room where some friends were still lingering, and shaking my head and crying. Thankfully, I didn't have to say the words. I didn't know what I was going to do with all of the grief I was feeling. In the early morning darkness, we made our last trip home from the hospital, a last caravan to our new reality.

Because Leah was an organ donor, we had to wait until her organs were harvested before her body was released. We did not realize at the time how difficult this would be. We were at home, numb with shock and grief, and we could make no plans. Our families and friends began arriving from out of town. Friends and neighbors arrived to rake our leaves, clean our house, and bring food. Dan went by the accident site and saw her friends gathering, and invited them to come over to our house. As her friends visited, we began to learn more about our daughter. We heard story after story of how she touched their lives.

Self-Care

Self-care is of the utmost importance at this time. When your grief is so raw that you don't know how you are going to make it through the afternoon, let alone go on to the next day, it's ok to start where you are. Listen to your body. If sleep evades you, rest. You may or may not feel like moving. Movement can shift your feelings, offering insight and integration. There is no right or wrong way to take care of yourself at this time. You can find a way to care for yourself that makes sense to you.

In those early days, tending to your basic needs may be all you can accomplish. Allow others to help you. Your friends will want to help anyway. Let them take care of basic chores so you can get the rest and sleep you need. Let them bring you a meal so you can have good nourishment. Let them sit with you, or bring you groceries. Your feelings of grief will remain, but when you are a little more rested and are eating even a little good, nourishing food, you may have a better capacity to be with your grief.

Chances are, your sleep has not been restful. Nap when you can, and listen to your body. You may be feeling grief and stress. You may be overwhelmed, or feeling everything all at once. Rest can very useful during this time. Slowing down and resting may bring up painful feelings, which is one reason we often try to get back to "normal," or what we used to know as normal, too soon. Taking time to feel your feelings, exactly as they show up each day, can seem daunting. Your feelings are so overwhelming that you don't know what to do with them. If you don't feel comfortable or safe doing this on your own, ask for support.

The Early Days of My Grief

I was wallowing in what felt like a deep pool of overwhelming feelings. I felt like I was drowning. I felt unable to connect with any rational thought. What do I do with the feelings that mired my days, my very existence? In the early days I vacillated between wanting to stop the feelings from coming, and letting them in. Either choice scared me. I wanted to put them somewhere so I didn't have to hear them, or see them, or feel them. There were so many questions. If I didn't feel them, what would happen? Will I stay in the dark place, where no light will ever shine again? If I stay here, can I lie down and go to sleep and not have to remember that my daughter died? That's what I wanted—to stay in a place where I didn't have to feel the pain, and didn't have to know if feeling my feelings would change my memories of my sweet girl.

What if I let them be? Allow my feelings in, allow myself to be with them. Do I dare feel them? If I feel them, will they spiral out of control and drive me mad, madder than I already feel? Or will they dissipate, change, shift? If they do, will that mean that I no longer grieve for my daughter?

I wish I had answers to those questions that made sense. Maybe that is the answer—that in early grief, there is no sense, no unraveling of the feelings that weighed me down, that threatened to tie me to the very bed that would not let me sleep each night. Maybe being in that fog, that soupy mixture of dread, utter sadness, despair, and agony that immobilized me was the beginning of finding my way out. Maybe not knowing how gave me a clue to living in the unknown.

I began to make time and space each day to feel my feelings exactly as they showed up. I created a safe place at the same time each day in which to be with my feelings. I took 1½-2 hours each day; you can spend the amount of time that feels right for you. In the early days, processing may not be possible and that is ok. I was scrupulously devoted to this practice every day for more than two years. The important piece here is consistency. When you know you will have the time you need to be with your feelings, at the same time each day, you may find it easier to get through days when you feel like you might fall apart. My clients also find this to be a very beneficial practice.

Things to Try:

In the early days of grief you may not know what to do. Here are some things that can help you.

1. Listen to your body. If you want to rest, give yourself permission to rest. If your body wants to move, listen to how your body wants to move. Your body has wisdom that will help you move through and integrate your feelings. This will change as you travel your journey.

2. Carve out some time each day to feel your feelings as they show up that day. Start where you are. If an hour feels like too much for you, start with five or ten minutes.

3. Make a list of self-care activities that nurture you, the basic things that you need right now. Revisit this list often to see what you can add, or what may change. Your list will help you when you can't readily think of what you need.

4. Grief is made up of many different feelings that arrive at different times with different intensities. It will help you to untangle your feelings, ask yourself what you are feeling in any given moment.

QUESTIONS FOR YOUR JOURNAL:

🍂 What were your initial feelings when grief entered your life?

🍂 In the early days of your grief, were you overwhelmed, feeling like you were drowning? What helped, or didn't help?

🍂 As you make time to be with your feelings each day, how have they changed or not changed?

🍂 What are you feeling now? And now? Continuing to ask this question can give you clarity.

Ten months since the accident.
Time is moving on, yet time seems different.
Not as many places to spread myself.
Certainly, I don't worry about Leah anymore.

—From My Journal, 9/3/2001

CHAPTER 3
Holding on to Who You Are

Natural Birth

My contractions began at 10:30 PM on April 27, 1983. It was my second pregnancy. Since my first pregnancy was delivered by cesarean section, I didn't know what to expect from my labor. My doctor told me to expect my labor to be much like a first pregnancy.

In 1983, a VBAC (vaginal birth after cesarean) felt like a revolutionary achievement. I gave birth to Leah naturally, without drugs and without intervention.

We had prepared for a natural birth in a birthing room, with midwives, when I was pregnant with my son in 1980. A car accident when I was 8 ½ months pregnant took away the hopes of a natural birth, and designated me "high risk" in the eyes of many of the doctors involved with my second pregnancy. Dan sustained injuries in the accident and was unable to be with me for Peter's birth. We were at separate hospitals, having separate surgeries; his to repair his heel, knee, and arm, and mine to have our baby. This experience was to be the first time Dan and I faced grief, early in our marriage. We grieved not only for the birth experience that we had planned together, but also faced our own injuries as we welcomed our son into our family and began our lives together. We had to give up the plans we had made for a very different kind of birth. We couldn't be the parents we wanted to be to Peter, at least at the beginning of his life. At the time, I recognized it as grief. Years later I wondered if it was yet another part of my preparation for my future work.

I sought out a VBAC support group during my second pregnancy, and we prepared for that. Since I was considered high risk, and had not yet met a homebirth midwife, I found a doctor in our group practice who was comfortable delivering my baby vaginally after having had a cesarean section. When I saw him on April 26th, a Tuesday, he told me that if I wanted him to be at my birth, I had to either have my baby the coming weekend or wait two weeks, as he was going on vacation the following Monday. Never one to put off until tomorrow what I could do today, I went home and did my pre-natal exercises, twice. Then I took a good long walk and told my baby that it was time for us to meet each other.

When my labor started that night, I stayed in bed to get some sleep for a while. I wasn't sure if I was really in labor. When I could no longer sleep restfully, I knew that I was having real contractions. I got up and began walking again, bringing my focus inside and breathing when contractions came. My contractions were the requisite five minutes apart by 7 AM. I had just come out of the shower when Dan woke up, and I told him it was time to go to the hospital. We hugged, dressed Peter, and headed out to drop him off at Grandma's as we made our way to the hospital, located in downtown Chicago, during rush hour. I felt calm. We had prepared well for this birth. I was the first time I had taken a stand for my body, and chose what was best for me and my baby.

I was admitted to the hospital and I gave them my birth plan, which my doctor had already signed. Dan and I were left alone for the most part, because as one of the attending doctors told us, "No one wants to be around when your uterus ruptures." My doctor had already assured me that he had been around long enough to know that uteruses don't just rupture, that and the knowledge I had from my VBAC group gave me the confidence I needed to relax and let my body do what millions of women have done before me—to give birth naturally. Dan and I walked the halls during most of my labor, me resting on his shoulders and going within when the contractions came. Through my birth plan, I agreed to be monitored once an hour for five minutes, so we always made sure we were in our room at the appointed time. We were told that they would not come to look for us, and if we weren't there then I would have the monitor on me for the duration of my labor. I progressed well and by late afternoon, I was fully dilated and ready to push. My doctor was there and had looked in on us a few times throughout the afternoon, so we headed to a delivery room.

I was on the delivery table with Dan behind me, supporting me with his strong presence in between contractions.

I soon had an undeniable urge to push. In awe of the power of that moment, I worked with my body to push out my baby, a girl, Leah. Our eyes locked in those first lucid moments. That moment is forever seared on my heart, those knowing deep eyes meeting mine for the first time, as if to say, "Ok, here we go." As if we both knew what lay ahead for us on our journey.

We continued to stare at each other as her dad cut the cord and handed her to me to nurse. Since she was born without drugs, we were both fully awake and fully present to each other. She latched on at once and began nursing immediately, assisting my placenta to be born. This birth experience did wonders to heal our first birth experience—the cesarean section, the birth that Dan was unable to attend. We longed for Peter to share in our joy. For the moment, though, it was the three of us getting to know one another. Dan and I smiled from ear to ear and held our beloved daughter.

Grief is Woven Throughout Our Lives

As I traveled my own journey and later began to help others navigate their journeys, I came to realize that grief is a lifelong journey. The first time we recognize grief may be when we lose a loved one. We often don't like to talk about grief; it brings with it so many connotations and taboos. It may bring with it shame and a sense of failure. It can bring us face to face with parts of ourselves that we would rather not see.

When we consider other kinds of grief and loss that we have experienced as a part of our lives, it can give context to the bigger griefs. You might think of it like a spectrum of grief and loss. When I grieved for the birth I wanted, it felt like a big grief at the time. I allowed myself to feel what I was feeling. Eventually, I was able to move through it. You may also discover parts of your grief wound that need further healing when you come upon another moment of grief in your life. For example, even though I was able to have the kind of birth I wanted with Leah, I was again reminded that I did have to make concessions because of my previous birth experience. You may discover that when a new loss occurs in your life, it brings up old or unresolved feelings of grief from a loss that you thought you had processed; you are given the opportunity to gain additional insight about both losses, and integrate the insight into your life experience.

The good news here is that your life always provides exactly the right opportunities for you to gain greater insight and deeper wisdom to assist you on your life journey. When we are faced with feelings from the past that we thought we were done with, we may think we are regressing, or that we have not come as far as we thought we have around a certain situation. Consider the opposite, that when a feeling spirals around again you are at a different place in your understanding of life, and you are given the opportunity to bring more profound healing to this place in your life. We sometimes turn away from the difficult times in our life for a variety of reasons. We don't like to be uncomfortable, we don't like to face the parts of ourselves that are difficult to love, or we want this phase of our life to be over without having to face our feelings or to do the inner work that comes at times of great challenge.

Preparation

Leah was intense from the moment she was born. Her intensity provided me with some of my biggest challenges from the moment she entered the world. She tested and tried all of her boundaries in a way that were joyous, tenacious, and wild. There are so many stories of her will to be herself, at every age. Even with my intention of meeting her where she was and for who she was, many battles ensued. My work in those days was to recognize the purity in her wildness and hold the space for her to expand. Neither of us understood her intensity. My fear was only overcome by the fear that I would hold her back. I knew what that felt like in myself, and it was not a pain I wanted to inflict on her. In meeting her, I was also able to meet myself in the raw and wild places that were never allowed to just be.

Leah taught me to fight for what was important. Just like fighting for the birth experience I wanted during my pregnancy, her birth ignited my fierceness. That fierceness served me well, not only as I mothered my children, but also as I began the journey as a daughterless mother.

Even before she was born, she was urging me to find my own way, to not settle for what was mainstream at the time, to look for ways to empower both of us to fight for what we wanted. I remember how radical it felt to find support for a VBAC, and how militant I felt gathering the information that would help us make the right choice for us. I remember how much resistance we got from our family and from some doctors, and how little that mattered when I surrendered to my inner knowing.

My journey through motherhood holds evidence of my fledgling attempts to use my intuition as I made the passage to my authentic self. As I reflect on my lessons of motherhood, my revelations are full of surprises. There is surprise that my children have been my biggest teachers. There is surprise that my mothering experience is nothing like I had imagined or expected it to be, as I took on the daunting task of nurturing two wonderful beings entrusted to my care. Peter and Leah were both beneficiaries of Dan's and my mission to change our personal family history. It was our conscious decision to allow our children to become the people they were meant to be, rather than trying to mold them into people we thought they should be. I share a very heart-warming relationship with my son, now a man. My mothering of him is complete, and the threads extending from my own inner work connect us as we continue an adult relationship that nourishes each of us.

Looking back on my journey as a mother, and the initiation of my daughter's death, I marvel at the ground I have covered. With Leah's life cut short, my true purpose had not yet been fulfilled when she died. I spent 17 ½ years helping her to learn the lessons she needed to learn in order to succeed in the world, and to become the person she was born to become. I often doubted the job I was doing, and was unsure of myself as we learned together. My lessons continued into the initiation of her death, and she helped me continue to acquire additional knowledge. As I contemplated the meaning of my life, and the high price I paid to continue the journey to myself, I began to excavate the qualities that would serve me well as I traveled along the path of my initiation, which led to the fullest expression of myself. I began to know my own power; the fear was no longer felt as fearful. My passion returned, and my doubt subsided. I knew who I was again. How my new life would manifest had not yet been revealed at the time of Leah's death, nor in the early years of learning to live without her physical presence in my life, but still I trusted. It was a deep, connected trust that continued to remind me that losing her was too high a price to pay to not live the life I was meant to live. The courage of my daughter continues to astound me. I have so much gratitude to Leah for choosing me to be her mom and for her part in our family. I know that all the times I doubted her and myself were invitations for growth. Her life had the potential to change the lives of everyone she touched.

I wanted to live my life with the lessons that her brave spirit left with me. It wasn't easy; each day challenged me in ways I never imagined. Each day the decision had to be made to accept that challenge. Yes, there are days I still cry. Sometimes it means staying home and crying while letting the feelings wash over me. Sometimes it means picking myself up and choosing to make my daughter proud of me, no matter how difficult that is on any given day. But to not live my life in the manner that Leah taught me would be to let her die in vain, and I refuse to do that. Sometimes I am surprised that I can still feel joy after having lost daily physical contact with my daughter.

I know that in the great cosmic mix of things, Leah and I agreed to this path to further our own spiritual growth. In the worst times, I wonder what kind a fool I was for agreeing to such a devastating role. Losing my daughter only to have to stay, live, and grieve for her forever after. Why me? I can feel such utter anguish on this lone path. After asking that for the millionth time, I return once again to my heart, my faithful heart, and know that I am on the right path. Along the way, I often did not know exactly what that meant. I sensed movement and I sensed an unfolding. When I was willing to be in each moment in my heart I was given, and continue to be given, possibilities for healing. I frequently wondered how a mother could heal after losing her daughter.

Fighting for What We Want

As human beings, we fight for all kinds of things. We fight for our point of view, and we fight for what we want. We may fight for what we don't want. Sometimes we have to fight for what is really important. We are reminded over and over at pivotal points, the importance of fighting for things that will make a difference in our lives. These reminders often arise from deep within us, and if we don't know what our intuition sounds or feels like in our bodies, we may ignore them or doubt them, staying in a more comfortable place or doing things the way we always have done them. What does it take for us to take up the fight?

The quest that I went on when I sought out a VBAC was spurred on by a deep desire to do what was best for my baby and me. My intuition told me there was a different way for me than to have a second cesarean section. Research and knowledge provided me with what I needed to continue to fight for what was right for both of us. It gave us the confidence to follow through despite what others may have thought about what we were doing.

Grief can provide one of these pivotal points in your life. The breaking open of your life by way of a loss can cause you to question your life in a way you never have before.

You may feel a deep urge for things to be different, or for things to be the way you always knew they could be. Grief can awaken your intuition, or it can be a training ground to acquaint yourself with the way your intuition shows up for you. You can gain confidence in allowing your instinct to guide you and lead you to a fight that is right for you.

Things to Try:

1. Make a list of all of your experiences of grief throughout your life. Notice how earlier loss may affect a later loss.

2. Is there a loss that does not feel complete on your list? Take some time to write about it. What were your feelings at the time of the loss? How have they changed now?

3. Plan a ritual to honor your losses. Choose one at a time, or several together.

QUESTIONS FOR YOUR JOURNAL:

- Answer this question for yourself. Losing _____ is too high a price to not be true to who I am.

- Have you ever felt that you settled for something, and then felt the pangs of grief and regret? List your "what if" and "if only" moments. Sometimes hearing or seeing them on the page can release the anxiety and fear.

- How do you find your fierceness of belief? Your path can change dramatically in view of loss. A step toward healing can begin the journey of discovery. What discovery are you longing for?

Today I got the insight that I still need to be where I am right now,
Which is different than where I was a year ago,
10 months ago, or even 6 months ago.
Wherever I am in any given moment Is where I need to be.

—From My Journal, 8/26/2001

CHAPTER 4
Practicing Radical Grief

Being Prepared

We are taught to be prepared from the time we are born. It's a Boy Scout motto; it may be a value in your family. We want to be prepared for every eventuality. It seems like the smart thing to do. Think of all the different ways we prepare during our lifetime. We go to school to help us learn the things we need to know to make our way in the world. We may take tennis, dance, or music lessons so we become more proficient in our chosen pastimes. We prepare for the births of our children. We prepare our children to start school, or to meet new members of the family. We prepare for exams, for job interviews, for big presentations, and for the holidays. There is no end to the role that preparation plays in our lives. The actual task of preparing for everything and anything that might come up in our lives can be a little crazy-making.

And yet, think of all the times you have said, "I wasn't prepared for that." It may very well have been the loss of a loved one, and it could have been something less impactful like a snowstorm, a traffic jam, or a cold. Sometimes the things we are unprepared for can turn into positive experiences, like a visit from an old friend or a letter giving us unexpected good news.

If you think about it, it is impossible to prepare for absolutely everything that occurs in your life. Even if it was possible, you would miss out on what is happening right now as you prepared for what was coming next. In order to live our lives to the fullest, we have to come to terms with preparing as best we can, and trusting that we will find what we need when the unexpected happens. Maybe a better way to think of it is that we prepare ourselves by trusting that we don't have to know it all at once; the unexpected occurrences in our lives is the training we need to learn how to live in the unknown, and how to be resilient when the unforeseen happens.

When we experience the unexpected loss of a loved one, our initial response may be of disbelief. Our experience not yet caught up with the reality of our loss. This is normal. One of the reasons we don't like to talk about grief is because of its unpredictability. Grief is not just one feeling; it is comprised of many different feelings. These feelings can be very intense and come at us all at once. We often don't know what to do with all of these feelings and we may not be ready for the physical manifestations of grief. We certainly may not know how to untangle our myriad feelings. Talking about our feelings can remind us that our reality has in fact changed, even if we are not prepared to face it. At this stage of grief we may prefer the distraction of our thoughts and denial of our feelings rather than risk the maelstrom of our emotions, and the reordering of our reality.

Laying the Groundwork

I awakened on November 9, 2000. Maybe "awakened" is not the right word, since I didn't really sleep after returning from the hospital in the wee hours of the morning. I tossed and turned in a sea of anguish, not wanting to surface completely because then I would be reminded that Leah was gone, but not wanting to give in to sleep completely because of the dreams that I feared. I stumbled out of bed, reality smacking at my face, tears coming now that couldn't be stopped. I went downstairs to Leah's room, shaking with convulsive tears. I looked at her clothes all over the floor, her bed unmade. I smelled her scent still lingering. Willow and Mabel, her dogs, were sleeping on her bed. They looked up at me with sad eyes. They, too, wondered where Leah had been, where she was now, when she would return to pet their fur and kiss their noses. I felt physically ill. I had no idea how I would go on. I cried silently for a few more minutes. Mabel and Willow ambled over, unsure of how to comfort me, asking in their own way, "Where is she?" I bent down and hugged them. They nuzzled my hair and licked my face, my salty tears mingling with what Leah fondly called their slobber. I gave both of them hugs, and they turned around to return to her bed. They were not ready to give up hope that their beloved girl would return soon.

As I turned around to go back upstairs, I heard this:

"Everything you have done up until this point has prepared you for what is next."

Saying that I heard it is not exactly true; it was a full body knowing. To this day, I remember exactly where I was and how I received that news. In that moment I had no idea what it meant.

I grew up feeling like I was different, like I was wrong, like I was never good enough. Throughout my life I have always been trying to fit in, to feel good enough, and to find my way. All of my searching led me to learn to follow my own intuition, to learn what that intuition feels like in my body, and to act on it with courage, I came to know this as my radical nature. I used to think a radical person was someone who did things completely against the norm, against the acceptable way to do them. Now radical is being me—being true to my authentic self, in alignment with the truth and essence of my soul. I love the word radical, and the energy it evokes for me. I relate to it, it feels comfortable in my bones.

My radical nature was pushed down and repressed as I was growing up, and not encouraged by my parents. My experience at the time is that my parents did not accept me for who I was, and contributed to my feelings of not belonging or being good enough. That single fact alone played a big part in my wanting to be there for my children in a way that I perceived my parents were not there for me. When Leah died, and I heard my inner knowing tell me that losing her was too high a price to pay to not be who I am, the enormity of that realization almost did me in. It made me want to curl up and stay right where I was, to hold my pain close to protect me from breaking out of that comfortable numbness.

Paying Attention

Have you ever found yourself in a situation that reminded you of an earlier thought? It may have felt more to you like a premonition. Is it possible for us to know that our experiences are in fact preparing us for a later chapter in our lives? I've pondered this thought, and here's what I can offer: The first few times—maybe even many times—this happens, we probably aren't aware that the experience we are having, or the thought that arises, is preparing us for something later in our lives. As we begin to travel our journey, though, we may remember something from the past that can help us with what may be happening in the present. When we begin to recognize this happening in our lives, it may not even be about a major life-changing event. Have you ever heard the phone ringing and known who was on the other end before you answered it? Or maybe you think about a person you haven't seen for a long time and you run into them that day or the next. These experiences are teaching moments; they are teaching us what our intuition feels like in our bodies, and how it shows up in our lives. Pay attention to how your body feels when you have an experience like this. Eventually you will begin to trust your feelings and begin to discern your intuition from your thoughts.

When you experience a great loss, some of these premonitions may return to your consciousness, like they did mine. You may remember a thought, a ritual, or a practice that is already a part of your life that can assist you now. Having a practice that is already a part of your life can give you a place to start when you encounter an unexpected life-changing event. This is a part of your preparation that is helpful to your life. Learning to live with the faith that your life's journey is beautifully orchestrated just for you, is all the preparation you will need to navigate through the trying—as well as the tranquil and joyous—parts of your life. Learning to recognize and embrace your intuition is an important part of this process.

Owning My Radical Nature

The way I met grief in the early days, and the way I continue to meet it, feels radical to me. It is radical in that it's not like anything else I have ever experienced, or any other way of coping I have heard of, although I admit I didn't want to look for any other way to meet grief than what I was drawn to instinctively. Learning how to follow my instinct and intuition has been a profound lesson for me.

What better way to learn that lesson than diving right into the middle of grief? Leah always did things her own way. Is it an irony that I protected her emerging and supported her to be her own person, and then I find myself doing the same for myself as I walked the rocky road of life after her death?

Is it radical to break a pattern? Is it radical to change the way my family history had progressed up until the time I was born? It breaks my heart to think that I was not able to do it until I had to face Leah's death. And yet, maybe the history was so entrenched in our generational story that nothing short of our journey together, including her death, could break that pattern.

Leah's birth was a radical act as well. She was there right from the start, helping me to discover and take a stand for myself, though I didn't even know it at the time. I could have distracted myself with stories of why she was really here—of how the intersection of our time here had a purpose—and pretended to know what that purpose was. If I did that, I would limit myself and what was possible for me, and I would limit the expanse of Leah's reach, too. I wanted to define it for both of us. I wanted to know for sure that there was a plan. There was, but it took a while for me to know the fuller story.

Parenting Leah was one of the most challenging experiences of my life. Early on in my grieving process I would often blame myself, rehashing not only the days leading up to the accident but also the conversations we had as we negotiated those thorny teenage difficulties. There were times when she would sneak out, and times I would sit up waiting for her, praying her safety and searching for a way to reach her that would break through her seemingly impermeable protective shell. Thinking about those times, I am sad that things ended when they did, and that I did not have more of an opportunity to know her longer.

We did talk, a lot—more than she said she wanted to talk. She often told me to leave her alone. As many mothers do, I balanced her need for independence and freedom with my need to give her direction and protection. It probably was not a realistic wish, to have long heart-to-heart discussions with a 17-year old daughter. In retrospect, it is hard to analyze a relationship cut short in the way ours was; she will always be 17 for me. I have much gratitude for the times we did have.

I now accept that the tough job I had with Leah—not just in her teen years, but from the moment she was born—was an essential part of my spiritual growth. When I look at it from a more global view, from the perspective of detachment, I can see how this is true.

From the day she was born, she was very intense and headstrong. She was her own person. When she looked into my eyes when she was just five seconds old, we just stared at each other. Maybe she still remembered where she came from. Maybe she was trying to communicate with those wise eyes something I was unable to comprehend. It was during those first few moments that I fell in love with her. The bond we formed on that first day was to carry us through the best times as well as the toughest times. As she grew she could delight—as well as exasperate—even the most patient of parents. I didn't claim to be one of those parents, but she provided me with many opportunities to become one.

I marveled at this independent little being. She always seemed to know more than I did. There was something about her eyes. She always was steadfast in her beliefs, even when I tried to steer her gently into looking at things from different perspectives. It was always her way. When she was two or three, our battles were around food. At seven or eight, she picked out her clothes and no one could convince her to wear anything else. It seemed like everything was a battle, especially with me. I took it personally at the time. I began to pick and choose my battles. She always ate, even somewhat healthily, as long as it was not my idea, and who cared if her outfits didn't match? She was expressing herself and she didn't seem to fight me as much when we were not fighting about everything. When she was not in a sulky mood, she was like the brightest light you could imagine, engaging everyone with her smile and beguiling ways.

As she became a teenager, our fights became more frequent. She became very sullen at times and absolutely refused to talk to me. She and I had many battles, sometimes leaving us both in tears. She wanted to be trusted, but like every normal teenager, she pushed that trust to its very limit and broke it several times. This is not about a laundry list of what she did; it is about me coming to terms with our relationship and broken trust, and the feeling that no matter what I did, I was not doing enough to keep her safe. A big part of my journey was surrendering to the fact that I didn't keep her safe. Ultimately, I couldn't keep her safe. I had to release the need to know why she died when she did.

She and I struggled enormously at times. I spent so much time trying to get through to her, trying to help her make good decisions, and I never felt like I was making progress. I always felt like my words were falling on deaf ears. My intent was to always honor her where she was in any given moment. I told her that so many times, that I always thought it was probably something she rolled her eyes at when she heard it. And yet every time we were able to connect after one of our tearful discussions, I could see the real Leah through the tough teenage façade. The light was there again, and I responded to it like everyone else did. I have thought many times since then that it must have been very difficult for her to live her life, not consciously knowing how short it would be, yet still feeling the urgent need to do the work she came here to do. It helps me understand her intensity, and the vague need she had to keep everything inside. So many times I felt hopeless, that I was not going to be able to reach her. That she truly did hate me. Accepting her where she was always brought huge surprises to me. She was much more and much less than the stories I had in my head about her. She was much more caring about her whole family, including me.

One time, as we were arguing, she had the presence of mind to stop, open the door to her room, and tell me, "Haven't you learned by now that I need to cool off before we can talk?" before slamming her door again. As I thought about what she had said, I remembered that if I left her alone in the heat of the argument, she would come to me later to talk. I was the one who needed an immediate resolution. She taught me the value of each of us taking some time to process what we were going through.

Another time, when I accused her of not listening to me, she said; "What makes you think I am not listening? I am not talking while you are."

In the summer before she died, there were hints of healing beginning. During the last three months of her life, she began to emerge. She was more often than not the light of our lives. She hugged me spontaneously more often. We had some really heartfelt talks. She spoke of missing my mom. I began to have hope that we were on the right track to get past the really tough times we had been through. She left before this happened completely. For a long time that haunted me. I thought back on all the arguments and all of the talks. Was it my fault that she died? What could I have done differently that would have changed the outcome? As I struggled with these thoughts, she began to let me know she was still around. I truly believe she accomplished what she came here to do. I believe that she is now doing important work wherever she is. But for so long, the pain of not resolving our differences before she left troubled me, and became another thing to surrender to the unknown.

What I do know is that if I did not have the experiences growing up that I did, I would not have had the same drive and radical urge to excavate my authentic self and then to be the kind of parent I was to my children. My feelings of being different served me well in my grief process and in how I live my life now. I have learned to embrace my differences. They make me who I am. My mother used to tell me that if everyone were the same, it would be a dull world. I never understood the magnitude of what she was telling me.

We often think our upbringing and our past is something we need to escape to become who we are meant to be. I have learned that our past is the perfect environment to cultivate the people we are meant to become—the people we already are.

Things to Try:

Here are some ways to help you see what your radical nature might look like.

1. As you begin to be aware of your intuition, pay attention to how your body feels. How does your intuition show up for you? How does your body feel? What sensations accompany your thoughts when you wonder if it is in fact your intuition?

2. Write about being prepared. What does it mean to you?

3. Think about what you turn to when you need to calm down or create space for yourself. Will this be useful for you when as you process your loss?

QUESTIONS FOR YOUR JOURNAL:

🍌 What were your first thought or feelings in the first days after your loss?

🍌 Have you ever had an Ah Ha moment that connected an event from your past with something that happened in the present?

🍌 How has one thing that you have done in the past prepared you for meeting your grief now?

🍌 Does something from your past that once seemed like an obstacle, now have a different feeling?

🍌 What is your radical nature?

🍌 Is there a word other than "radical" that better describes your true essence?

It is 8 months after Leah died.
I have experienced feelings I never knew existed.
Grieving for my child has been different than I ever expected.

—From My Journal, 7/10/2001

CHAPTER 5

Grieving Uniquely

How We Grieve

If you have been on your own grief journey, you know firsthand that we all grieve as uniquely as we love the person we have lost. We can easily agree that our love for the people in our lives is as unique as the relationships we have with each of them. Each person's personality, nature, and temperament plays a part in the makeup of the love we share. So it stands to reason that not only does every person on the planet grieve in his or her own unique way, but that each of us may also grieve for different people in our lives in different ways.

We have all heard about different phases and stages of grief. On the continuum of grief, these stages can show up differently not only for each of us, but also for each person we grieve. Some of us may skip stages altogether, some people stay in denial, and some people never reach a certain stage. Some people start with acceptance; some never get to it. You get the idea—your own template for grieving is as distinctive as your fingerprint.

A lot of experts have studied grief. Researchers, doctors, and spiritual teachers, to name a few, have historically been intrigued about how human beings grieve one another. Swiss psychiatrist Elisabeth Kübler-Ross, in her 1969 book, *On Death and Dying*, describes it as these 5 stages: denial, anger, bargaining, depression, and acceptance. Other sources names seven stages of grief, and others even more. Dr. Kübler-Ross noted, later in her life, that the stages are not a linear and predictable progression, and that she regretted writing them in a way that was widely misunderstood. Rather, they are five of the common experiences that the bereaved can experience, and can be experienced in any order, if at all. As grief continues to be studied and is better understood, the way we travel through it gains clarity.

My own experience is that there are numerous stages and phases of grief. They are not linear, and you don't progress through them in any particular order. They can feel chaotic and they can revisit you time and time again. In early grief, there is no pattern or form to these feelings and stages. Eventually, I began to describe my experience as a spiral of grief. You will find words and structure to describe your journey as you go through it.

Some of the ways I have felt or acted in my own journey were shock, denial, fear, panic, guilt, hurt, pain, loneliness, bargaining, depression, hopelessness, anger, emotional outbursts, isolation, adjustment, hope, trouble with the "new normal," new strengths, courage, adjustment, and acceptance. This is not at all a complete list. My husband Dan wrote about feeling like he was "grieving bravely." If you acknowledge your feelings when they show up, they won't have to get louder in order to get your attention.

Leah's friend Matt shared this with us shortly after he returned home from the funeral:

> *"But the suddenness of Leah's (death) shocked me into remembering that none of us are immune. Death can happen to anyone, at any time. Like dust on the wind, we can be gone, without a second thought. I hope she knows that as tragic as the events were two weeks ago, Leah changed my life. I am not ready to die, and I by no means want to die, but I am not afraid of it. I also hope that if, God forbid, something were to happen to me in the near future, she would be the first person I see."* —Matt

Laughing and Crying

We were sitting in the hearse going to the graveyard from the church. I looked around at Dan, at Peter, and at Leah's friends who were pallbearers. In that moment everything was surreal. This one event brought these people together in one place. No other circumstance could have done that. I began laughing hysterically. I couldn't stop myself. I held Kleenex over my face and I was confident that hysterical laughing looked the same as crying, so I let myself laugh. There was no stopping it anyway; it was an unseen force in my body. The laughter eventually changed to crying. No one knew the difference. What is it that makes us laugh or cry about something? I didn't find my daughter's funeral funny. I found it peculiar to be sitting in a hearse with her friends without her being there. And there was something about being at her funeral without being able to tell her about it that cracked me up. I saw the flash of a headline, "Mother Laughs Hysterically at Her Own Daughter's Funeral," and pictured the tsk tsk of the readers; that made me laugh even harder. This was the first indication to me that I was not a conventional griever.

As days turned to weeks, and then months, the nightmare of missing my daughter refused to go away. At first I found myself marking time by the milestones of days. Fridays brought me back to the day of her accident. Fridays had the power to pull me into a vortex of regret. I replayed the days leading up to that fateful day, examining each conversation, pulling them apart and looking for that one place I could have changed the outcome of that day.

The weekends offered respite from the daily normal and our feeble attempts of going on with our lives, trying to do the things we always did—our jobs, church, and daily chores. I always fell short of reentering the normal or of making sense of my life without my daughter's physical presence. The weekend afforded more space and time. I collapsed into the safety of my isolation, not needing to be anything other than a mother missing her daughter. The space and time allowed more feelings to come up. When I allowed myself to feel them, sometimes the grip on my tender heart relaxed just a little.

When I couldn't feel them, I continued the suffering that Fridays tossed me into.

Mondays had the flavor of emerging from a deep dark hole. Mondays offered new beginnings. Each Monday my daughter was still not there, and I again started attempting to fit into my new reality, a reality not of my choosing.

I went through this cycle each week, until I was measuring time in terms in months—one month since Leah's been gone. Two months. I wondered if I was doomed to mark my days from here until eternity in terms of Leah's absence from my life.

I noticed a shift—ever so slight—at six months. I felt a deep sense of connection to Leah, and I felt her trying to comfort me in my grief, to encourage me to let go of past hopes and dreams in order to make space for what comes next. I had a sense of the collective energy field and how it supported me and gave me what I needed when I needed it. I tried to describe my grief in words. It felt raw and huge and jagged and relentless. When I stayed completely in it in my heart, I got past the fear and panic of her not being there, and the energy shifted and I felt grace and support. I could see it symbolically, at times, for a moment, and those were moments of true clarity. I felt like I was the vessel keeper for gifts from my mom, grandma, and Leah, who all were no longer physically here. I was in awe and honored to receive them.

After eight months, grieving for my child remained different than I ever could have imagined. I was letting go of expectations. I didn't consider myself an expert, but I knew myself well enough to know that I must grieve in my own way. I let go of expectation. Not too long before, I was learning to let go of an independent teenage daughter who was almost ready to leave for college. As a parent, I always felt that the letting go process began at the moment of conception. As soon as my body was ready to accept an embryo to nurture for nine months, it began the process of getting ready to let go; the embryo grew into a fetus and then finally a baby ready to be birthed into the world. As soon as I accepted my baby into my arms, I too began letting go, little by little. I always knew that the steps of growth, from infancy on, were preparing me to let go. I always thought that I would be letting go of my attachment to my child so that she could become the person she was born to be—and I was. I just didn't think it would be so absolute. I didn't think I would have to let go of her physical self. She did become the person she was born to be in this world. What parent would ever think that her child's role in life would be complete by the time she was 17, and then she would be gone? It's just a clear sign to me that letting go of our children and expectations is an ongoing lesson and sometimes a challenge. Letting go is a daily progressive process. I always felt that if I let go in appropriate ways, day by day, that I would be ready to let go when the time came. I was thinking more of leaving home for college, however, and not leaving this world for the next.

When my son left home for college, I cried easily the whole summer before. We had a ritual to mark his leaving home. Even though I had let go little by little up until this time, it was still hard to see him leave. To not have him living with us daily was a change for all of us. Leah told me that I still had her, and I told her that it was now her turn to be an only child for a while. We all missed Peter, and we all helped each other adjust. Leah told me after Peter had been gone for a while that she did not like being an only child. She missed him being a part of her daily life, and even though she knew he had to be in college, she wanted him back. She called him often to keep him updated on family matters.

How could any of us had known that less that three short years later I would be saying the exact same words about Leah, with a completely different meaning? We did adjust to Peter's leaving, and we all became comfortable with our new routine. When we were together there was much laughter. Peter and Leah became much closer. I loved these family times. I felt confident that when it became time for Leah to leave for college, that I would handle it much better. I even began to look forward to that time. I saw it as the next stage in our lives. Dan and I would be empty nesters. We saw a light at the end of the tunnel. We would have more time to devote to ourselves. We were looking forward to having adult relationships with both Peter and Leah. And then Leah left in a different way, her own way; it was the ultimate letting go experience for a parent. How could I do it? I was willing to let go of my children to go to college, to leave home to begin lives of their own—but how could I let go of Leah forever?

After Leah died, Peter told me that he did not want to be an only child. How could these two events, leaving for college and leaving this earth, both carry the same words and feelings? These were only a few of the questions I was facing. *Why*, was the most pressing. Why did this happen? How could this have happened to my daughter, my larger than life, very much alive, daughter? How and why? I knew that these questions could not be answered. I must let go of needing to know the answers to these questions. I knew that it was all a part of the mystery of life and death. I knew that my hopes and dreams and expectations for Leah and our lives together would have to die, too. And I knew, even in the first instant of grief for her, that by surrendering I would make space for new blessings. Even when I was faced with something as devastating as losing my child, I trusted that basic truth. I am sure I didn't realize it at the time, but that too was a blessing. I'm not sure, even today, what a conventional griever is, but it felt like I was doing things differently than the norm.

Permission to Grieve

Give yourself permission to progress through grief in whatever way makes sense to you. The key is that you will get through it. Your life may not look the same as it did before, but when you find the willingness, courage and resolve to face your uncomfortable feelings you can find meaning and purpose in your life again. Sometimes knowing that you have permission to move through your journey at your own pace can help you to relax. When you are relaxed, your stress level drops, and when you are less stressed the experience of your grief can be less overwhelming and feel a little more manageable. When you have permission to walk your own walk, you find the resilience you need to traverse the rockier parts of your journey.

You may also find yourself on the receiving end of advice that does not feel good to you, or people may say things to you that are not helpful. Many times people are well-intentioned with advice, but they too are uncomfortable and don't know what to say.

Take the time to honor what feels right to you. Seek out support that resonates for you. This may be the time to develop your fledging intuition, or return to it; ask inside what is right for you.

Your intuition can be a great inner guide when you are grieving.

It is also important for you to feel safe while you grieve. Spend some time thinking about, or writing about, what you need to feel safe. For some, it may be another person to witness your feelings. Others may need solitude and quiet. You will probably need some of each at different times in your journey. This is an important part of self-care while you are grieving. Let others know what you need.

Does talking about your loved one brings you comfort? If so, find someone who is willing to listen without offering their advice or judgment.

You may want to write about your feelings or express them in a collage or artwork. Collage can be a great way to get in touch with your feelings when you're not ready, or are unable, to express them in words.

If you prefer to keep your feelings to yourself, let those around you know that you don't want to talk about what happened right now. At some point you may want to talk about your memories. You are the one who can set the boundaries on your own grief journey.

The Portal Opens

As I progressed day by day I faced my feelings as they arose. I processed my grief through Samyama, a heart-centered direct experience practice that helped me to be with my feelings, with the guidance of my Samyama practitioner. Through the years, she had extended an invitation to me to experience the Temple of the Sacred Feminine, where she learned Samyama firsthand. Until Leah died I always felt intimidated, feeling that I was not far enough along on my spiritual path to attend. Actually, I was scared. After Leah died I was still scared, yet somehow I knew instinctively that this was the right path for me.

Up until that point my intuition was in its fledgling stage. I mistrusted it more than I trusted it. Losing Leah reframed many things, my fear included. It dismantled my life. I was at an intersection, a crossroad. It was a place that was completely different than the way my life was before. I could have gone any of several ways. I could have stayed where I was, and become frozen into a version of myself that was unrecognizable, immobilized in pain and denial. I could have lamented my situation, and again stayed stuck in a living hell. My daughter's legacy urged me on. I took on my grief moment by moment in a way that made sense only to me. It became a journey and initiation, a deconstruction and reconstructing of a life. My grief journey provided me with an opportunity to align more fully with my truth and my values. Many times along this path I wished that I had chosen one of the other paths. It seemed easier to lament my misfortune, numbing my pain with distraction and staying stuck, in a place that allowed me relief from knowing the reality of life without my daughter.

She wouldn't let me, though. She always came through when I was at my lowest, with a message, a song, or a blessing that reminded me that my work was yet to be revealed, and the way through it was by feeling everything as it arose. What I didn't know at the time is that I was defining my future work by my own grief journey. My initiation was taking me through rigorous inner work. It was a training ground on which to learn the work I would bring to others. I gestated this work in the Temple of the Sacred Feminine. The Temple provided me with a mentor, a community of women, and an atmosphere of love that allowed me to transform into the person that I am and always have been. It reminds me that I am the one I've been waiting for, to paraphrase our Hopi Elders. It was a discovery, a recovery, a metamorphosis, and an excavation. It was alchemy.

It was here that I learned to trust my intuition implicitly. I learned how to live from the lens of my heart; I learned that my heart can hold what my head can't understand. I learned how to be with all of my feelings, the comfortable and the not-so-comfortable. I learned how to hold space for others by learning to hold space for myself. From this place I continued to get glimpses of my future work. I knew that it would look different than I thought it would, different than anything else around. I grew to trust that I would recognize it when I was ready. I entered Samyama apprenticeship and became a Samyama practitioner long before I fully stepped into my work supporting others on their grief journeys. It was a long, lonely road at times; I was living in the unknown, just trusting that I was on the right path. As I traveled further on the spiral of my grief journey, I saw that each turn of the spiral brought, and continues to bring, new insights.

Peter, Dan, and I each dealt with grief in our own way. Each one of us somehow had the wisdom to know that we had to attend to our own needs first. We could not comfort each other until we learned how to comfort ourselves.

In the first few years Dan and I did most of our grief processing in private. We were too vulnerable to grieve together. We could talk about Leah and talk about our process, but we each needed to find our own way to meet our grief.

Once we emerged from the day-to-day shock of losing Leah, we then came smack up against places in ourselves and our marriage that were not serving us. This initiation was all-encompassing. If we were on a road to better versions of ourselves, we were being given the chance to examine all areas of our lives. Once we began processing our grief together, and were willing to be vulnerable with each other, all the things we had been avoiding while we raised our family came to the surface. We began a multi-year process of sitting with all that arose. We discovered we were no longer willing to just coast in our relationship. Our experience was calling us to a deeper intimacy with each other and ourselves. If our relationship was to survive losing our daughter, the parts of our marriage that were not working also needed to be examined, deconstructed, and rewoven into a partnership that served and nurtured each of us separately as well as together. During this time we often did not know if our marriage would survive. The process of meeting the grief of losing Leah brought up other disappointments and unresolved issues. We began to learn firsthand that grief weaves its way into aspects of our lives where we never expected to find it. As we made our way through this difficult time, we held a ritual to surrender all that was no longer serving us in our relationship.

At our ritual we made an intention for the next part of this journey; our intention was to enter into a Sacred Partnership. We spent two more years learning how to rise from the ashes of two hurt people who missed their daughter dearly, but who also had a deep desire to create a meaningful life together. This was a very uncomfortable and painful time. We were no longer willing to make due or settle for less that we both knew was possible. We spoke our intent to meet each other from our own truth and integrity, each bringing a whole person to the other, rather than looking to the other to make us complete. After two years of prayerful sitting, together and alone, we recommitted to each other at sunrise on a beach in Cozumel.

Today, we continue our journey by first tending our own soul work, and then meeting each other consciously in each moment as it arises, rather than by bringing up stories from our past or by fabricating new ones. When we find ourselves getting lost in the stories, we now have the skills to unravel them.

Learning how to honor each other's grieving process was integral in creating a relationship that allowed each of us the room to grow, both together and individually.

These days, we do not begin any important conversation without first sitting in silence with our intentions in our hearts. The outcome is always without attachment of how we are going to get there. It is amazing to me where these explorations take us after we sit.

Things to Try:

A few things to help you learn to recognize how you grieve.

1. Make a collage to express your feelings. Go through magazines and cut or tear out pictures, words, and phrases that speak to you. They don't necessarily have to remind you of your loved one. Gather your pictures, words, paper, scissors, and glue sticks. Sit in silence, or listen to a song that has meaning for you and your loved one. Begin to make your collage, choosing your pictures and words without a lot of thought—just use what you are drawn to in each moment. You can also add paint or marker to your collage.

2. Keep a journal of your feelings on a daily or weekly basis. This will let you track your feelings, and can be a great help and companion on your journey.

3. Look at other areas of your life. Are there places that need some attention? Are there places you've neglected? Take some time to examine these places and see what is needed for further integration or healing. Consider creating a ritual to honor a part of life that no longer serves who you are now.

QUESTIONS FOR YOUR JOURNAL:

- How do you grieve?
- Do you grieve differently for different people in your life you have lost?
- Are there unresolved issues that need attention?
- What do you need to feel safe?
- How can you connect with family members who may be having a different experience of grief than you are?

Remember to listen to the Language of your Heart.

—From a Samyama Session, 3/1/2016

CHAPTER 6
Opening Your Heart

Entering the Gate

"Leah died. I need an appointment." I spoke these words to my long-time Samyama practitioner shortly after Leah's death. I was the one speaking, but I felt like I was seven years old. I felt lost and alone, and scared. I felt like I was missing a part of myself. I knew I had to reach out and get help, so I made the appointment, but each time I saw the date, I wanted to cancel it. How could anyone else help me? How could anyone else know what I was feeling?

On the day of my appointment, I both dreaded and looked forward to going. I hadn't seen my Samyama practitioner, D, in a while, but I was grateful that I had an established relationship with her as my practitioner. I had been working with her on and off for almost seven years. She taught me Samyama in our early years of working together, but I have never used it for such a big issue, or for such intense feelings. Samyama was first described in the Yoga Sutras of Patanjali, compiled around 400 CE. He defined it as the practice of concentration, meditation and the perception of who you are and how you believe the world to be. In practice, Samyama is far simpler than the description.

I knew that I couldn't process my grief on my own. I knew I needed help.

I parked my car in front of the building she occupies. There it was, the wrought iron gate. The first time I saw that gate, when I first started coming here, I knew I was in the right place. The design of the gate, what looked like intertwining hearts beckoning to mine, first showed up in a dream many years ago, and seeing its familiar design gave me courage. As I opened the gate, I had a feeling of rightness. I was not alone. It felt like I was opening the gate to hope. But when I opened the door to the studio and walked down the stairs, I was gripped by fear. I wanted to run away before she saw me. And then she opened the door. I was standing in the middle of the room, willing myself invisible. She saw me, welcomed me, hugged me, and we entered her office.

As I sat down, she said, "I am so honored to walk with you on this journey."

I gulped, and tears started running down my face.

"I invite you to close your eyes and begin breathing, slowly."

I noticed I was holding my breath, so I began to breathe.

"Slowly, slowly, bring your breath to your heart center."

I remembered how to do this; I closed my eyes, placed my hand on my heart and began to deepen my breath. I brought my awareness to my heart. On that day I was grateful to have my hand there to help me find focus.

"What are you experiencing in your heart, Nancy?" Her voice is calm and loving.

I went to my head; I didn't want to feel what I was feeling.

"When you find yourself returning to your thoughts, bring your focus back to your heart on your next breath."

I breathed myself back to my heart. I stayed there a moment longer this time. My feelings of sadness and loss swelled in my heart, and my tears flowed once again.

"What are you aware of in this moment, Nancy?" her soothing voice asked once again.

I croak, "It hurts, so much."

"Yes. Is there another feeling you are feeling along with the hurt?"

"Pain in my heart. My heart hurts. I feel so sad."

"Can you allow the feeling of sadness to be there as it is?"

I took in her words. That was my fear—that I would have to feel the pain as it was. My head began telling me, *If only I had not gone to work that day, if only I had been a better mother, if only…*

"What are you experiencing in this moment, Nancy?"

I managed to choke out, "All the things I should have done to keep this from happening. All the things I did wrong as a mother."

"Can you bring that story to your heart? Can you allow yourself to feel the feelings without the story?"

I dropped the story of my inadequacy to my heart.

"Give it lots of breath."

I breathed into my heart. I felt myself going deep into my heart, feeling the spaciousness that was there and allowing myself to feel the sadness and pain of not being able to hug or see Leah. I was able to do it; I was able to feel the feeling without the story. I felt my heart breaking open, and wave upon wave of pain, sadness, and loss emanating from it as tears streamed silently down my cheeks. At some point, D asked me if she could touch my arm, and she moved closer and placed her hand there. I felt her support as I continued to sit with all of my feelings, allowing them to be there as they appeared, allowing them to crash from my heart into the field of love that I felt.

After that, I looked forward to my Samyama sessions. As painful as they were, I was able to go much deeper and feel much deeper with D than I could on my own. My daily time to feel my feelings was still important, and now that I started processing my grief with D, I felt the shift in my feelings in a much more profound way.

A Portal to Your Deepest Feelings

Samyama allows us slow down, make space, and pause. Whenever we do slow down, our feelings can surface, letting themselves be known and felt more intensely. When this first starts to happen, especially when we are in the throes of grief, it can feel too vast for us to take on. It is important during times like this that you seek help, finding someone who can help you hold space for your feelings to be felt at their fullest. It is also comforting to know that Samyama can be a resource for every aspect of your life. It can help you be with whatever you are feeling, and can assist with the full spectrum of life experiences, from everyday disappointments like sitting in traffic, missing an appointment, or having disagreements with family members or co-workers, to bigger, life-changing events, or tragic or devastating ones. Samyama can even teach you how to hold joyful feelings in your heart so that you can fully embody those feelings as they are.

A Samyama practitioner can teach you how to hold space for yourself, bringing a new dimension to your practice. Self-Samyama is available to you every day. The more you practice, the deeper you will go into your heart— into the mystery. Your own self-Samyama practice will allow your facilitated sessions to be even deeper.

Unraveling Stories

I remember a particularly powerful session we had a few years into my journey.

As I sat down in the chair, I closed my eyes, placed my hand on my heart and began to breathe. I knew what to do, and I got right to it.

"What is in your heart today, Nancy?"

I dropped deeper in my heart. I allowed what was there to arise. A cold fearful dread arose in my heart. I remembered the drive to the hospital and the fear of entering Leah's room after her surgery. I remembered seeing her broken body, and touching and stroking her cheek and her head. I remembered how upset she began to get as she woke up from surgery, before she was put in a medically induced coma. I remembered...

"What are you experiencing in this moment Nancy?" D's soothing voice interrupted my reverie.

Through my tears I managed to squeak out, "The accident, the time in the hospital, the..."

"Bring those stories to your heart. What are you feeling there, in your heart?"

By now I am crying loudly. "Sad... devastated... so raw. It hurts so much."

D had moved closer, so she could rest her hand on my arm. "Are you willing to feel your sadness as it is, right now?"

My head screamed, *No! What good will that do?* But I managed to say, "I'm willing to be willing..."

"Good, bring your willingness to feel your sadness and pain to your heart."

Even though I had been feeling the sadness and pain in my heart for some time now in my Samyama sessions, this time felt harder, more intense, and completely overwhelming. Little by little I did; I allowed myself to feel the sadness and pain, easing into it a little more with each breath. My thoughts were on a rampage, looking at every little detail of the hospital stay, remembering...

"Are you in your head?"

I managed to nod my head yes.

"Take a big breath and bring your awareness back to your heart, to your willingness to feel your sadness and pain as it is in this moment."

I take a breath and return to my heart, feeling the enormity of the sadness there, tears continuing to stream down my face. The feeling gets bigger, and bigger, and just before it feels like it is going to consume me, it diminishes; just a little at first, then like a wave crashing on the shore.

"What are you experiencing now, Nancy?"

I was able to take a deeper breath. I breathed in deeply— more deeply than I had been able to breathe for months. I stayed in my heart. The feelings were softer, and for the first time I felt safe to feel them.

" There are no words for how I feel. I want to stay with this feeling," I said.

The intensity of my sadness and pain seemed to take on a different quality on that day. The incessant stories my mind liked to spin calmed a little, and I could be with the sadness without thinking about all of the "what-ifs" and "if-onlys." I could do this. I could be with the pain and sadness and all the other feelings that came if I held them in my heart. I understood what it meant to say that my heart could hold the feelings as they are without wanting or needing them to be different.

My head has a field day with that. *What do you mean you don't need things to be different? You don't want Leah back?* it asked.

Of course I do, but she is not here.

I returned to my heart. I didn't understand how this worked— how I could feel the most devastating pain in my heart, yet want to stay there. All I knew was that it was better than the constant suffering brought on by hearing my thoughts, over and over again, regurgitate past events that couldn't be changed.

"What is in your heart in this moment, Nancy?"

"I am feeling gratitude."

WHAT? my head screamed.

I noticed that thought, and brought my awareness back to my heart. "I am feeling gratitude for this work. For the capacity of my heart to hold my feelings, to be able to feel them as they are without suffering."

"Can you find a way to bring yourself back to that place when the stories come back?"

"Yes, I can."

With that, our session was over. I wanted it to last longer—forever. As I left, I was filled with the wonder of the experience, of the nuances of Samyama. Yes, I was grateful for the work. With that session I understood that the experience of Samyama deepens each time we enter the space of our heart. I understood what it meant that the present moment holds everything we need. I knew it in a way I didn't know it before.

Samyama had been a part of my life for almost seven years before Leah died. I was very familiar with its subtle power, and yet I used it sparingly until then. Each time I turned to it in the years before Leah died, I was always amazed at the insights and the calm I experienced from its practice. When I began to use it to process my grief, I recognized several things. First, it held potential to shift my feelings of grief in a profound way. Second, I experienced the heart as an alchemical vessel and what it means for the heart to hold everything.

Samyama as a direct experience practice means that there are no words to describe how it works or what it does, and so I offer this glimpse into my sessions for the reader:

> *Samyama, for me, is the connection to my soul and intuition. It brings me into contact with the field of all possibility, the unknown, and the mystery. As I continued my journey I became more comfortable with the unknown and more familiar with the mystery, which is to say I surrendered to both.*

Even though Leah's death was my portal into living daily in my heart, Samyama affected every other aspect of my life. Through Samyama I was able to access a part of my self that I never could before, my inner child self. The key was allowing her to feel what she was feeling in the moment. I had done inner child work many years before, but never with the feeling part. By allowing my little girl to feel what she was feeling, no matter what age she appeared in a given moment, I was able to meet parts of myself that I had never met before. I knew they existed, but only under the guise of fear, or anger, or some other way of acting out, getting my attention, or trying to control outcomes. Samyama was the key that unlocked access to myself; for the first time I was coming face to face with myself. When I was able to relate to myself, listen to myself, and allow myself to feel, all of my relationships with others began to change as well. It was not that I was changing them; rather, my attitude was changing as I integrated parts of myself that had been in shadow. When I began meeting these shadow parts of myself in my heart, they were great teachers. I learned firsthand that all parts of us want to be met; Samyama gave me the skill to meet them as they are in my heart.

After Leah died, I knew intuitively that Samyama was the only thing that would take me from one moment to the next, through my pain and despair and grief. It was part of the preparation that I had done that would serve me along my grief journey and guide the work that came after Leah died. I dove into it, still wanting things to be different, but at the same time knowing that the only way through this was to be with the pain, devastation, and grief as each appeared in each moment. It was not easy, but I came to know it was necessary. This was not a conscious, well thought out analytical decision; it was a heart decision, and it was almost choiceless.

Other Ways to Open Your Heart

Living with an open heart is one of the best ways I know to learn how to feel your feelings. In addition to Samyama here are some of the other ways I've found to be heart opening:

- Embodiment—to live in and be aware of your body. There are many ways to be embodied: Samyama, or another type of meditation; yoga, or another kind of movement that brings you into awareness of your body. We often are not aware of our bodies and do not live in them.

- A walk in nature, or being in nature.

- Deep abdominal breaths.

- A hug.

- Sharing time with a loved one.

As you can see, there are many ways to open your heart, and you can probably think of a few more. You may also see the resemblance to self-care, and that's because self-care is heart-opening. Self-care deserves another mention here because it is the nourishment that opens your heart.

Things to Try:

We often aren't aware of the transformative power of our heart. You can begin to explore your own. How do you know if Samyama is right for you?

1. Take a moment to close your eyes and become aware of your breathing. Allow it to deepen and become slower with each breath. Breathe deep into your abdomen. Stay with your breath for now, just breathing into your belly, knowing there is nothing else to do in this moment.

2. Start slow, the first few times you practice. Do only this breathing for as long as you are comfortable. Each time you do it, you can go a little longer. Right now I want you to become used to being quiet in this way. In our busy lives, even before grief steps in, we rush around, fearful of slowing down and being quiet because we don't want to face our feelings.

3. After you have become used to being quiet, the next step is to bring awareness to your heart. Take time to establish your slow, deep abdominal breath. After a time, place a hand on your heart and direct your attention to your heart space, the center of your physical heart. Breathing and softening with each breath, there is nothing to do in this moment. Continue to breathe and be in your heart. When you find yourself in your head, notice your thoughts and return to your heart. This is the practice of Samyama; continuing to return to your heart each time you are in your head. We are not trying to get rid of thoughts; we notice them and return to our heart on our next breath.

4. What else opens your heart? Continue to add to your list as you make new discoveries.

QUESTIONS FOR YOUR JOURNAL:

- How do you feel when you think about slowing down?

- Are there any feelings that feel too big or scary to allow into your heart?

- When do you feel most embodied? Are you aware when you are not embodied? How do you know?

- What happens when you pay attention to a feeling that is trying to get your attention? What happens when you ignore the feeling?

I stand at the edge of nothingness. I have lost my daughter.
My Grief wraps around me like a warm cloak.
Sweet comfort, it defines me.
My pain sears through me I know I am alive.
Through the darkness, a glimmer of light?
No it can't be, my daughter is dead
but it won't be denied, this growing light, I shield my eyes,
I do not want to see, I want to stay in the grief,
in the pain, my Pain.
It serves me well, my daughter is dead,
reason enough to stay here, to wallow in the muck,
in the burning fire of my torment.
The light grows, I open my eyes and shut them against the glare, I am not yet
ready to face clarity, to know the reason I am left,
left to pick up the pieces of my shattered life,
dreams around my feet like a million shards of glass.
Tattered reflections of the remnants of my life
destroyed in an instant, by cosmic design.

—From My Journal, 4/2003

CHAPTER 7
Renovating the House

Your Life is Like Your House

In the wake of grief you are going to do some renovation— renovation to your life, and maybe even renovation to your house. Let me tell you what we did.

Torn Apart

Our house was literally and completely torn apart. What started as a leak in the master bathroom turned into a major renovation. Our entire kitchen and former dining room were torn down to the studs. We were living in two rooms of our house; our refrigerator was in the living room. We had been eating out for too long. Our torn-apart house felt like my torn-apart life. The physical ripping apart of our lives was as excruciatingly painful as the emotional devastation. We found drawings of Leah's in the back of drawers—more reminders that she was once here, but no longer. I wondered if anything would ever seem normal again. Would everything always be overshadowed by Leah's absence?

Our house would be finished, eventually. It would be better than it was before—bigger, and more beautiful. Could I say the same thing about my life? Were we renovating our entire house to avoid our feelings of grief? The renovation was taking its toll on us. It went on longer than we thought it would, dust was everywhere, and we were tired of the disruption. In a way it did feel like our grief; it felt like it would never end.

In the middle of all the disruption, I was inspired to paint, and I wondered where it came from. I hadn't painted for a long time—at least since before Leah died, maybe longer. What was I going to paint? Better question: what would I paint on? The need to paint was urgent. I walked around the house, looking for paper. I walked into the kitchen, or what would be the kitchen, and saw the studs and the back of the living room drywall. I heard myself say, "That's it! I'll paint the studs and behind the wall!"

It was brilliant. I hadn't felt that excited about anything since… Wait. A feeling of horror—I felt excited? I felt inspired? How could that be? My daughter was dead. That right there was a good enough reason to never feel good or happy or excited again. *No,* I told myself, *I can't paint the walls, it wouldn't be right.* But as that thought passed through my mind, I found myself putting water in containers, squeezing paint on my pallete and setting brushes out. And I started painting. I painted all of our names on the drywall: Dan, Peter, Leah, Nancy; our pets, Willow, Mabel, Oreo. I wrote, "Our hearts are forever connected." I painted free form shapes, whatever I was inspired to paint. I painted the studs, too. I left a mark on the house.

I felt so free—more like myself than I had since… Oh no, there it was again. What was happening? I sat down and looked at my paintings. It felt somewhat risqué to be painting the walls, even though they would be covered up. If I felt like myself, did that mean I was healing? If I healed, did that mean I'd forget about Leah? That she wouldn't be a part of my life anymore? What does healing from the death of my daughter mean, anyway?

Those questions haunted me. If I were to be honest, they had been haunting me for some months. At the beginning of this renovation, on Leah's 20th birthday, I received the inspiration that Leah's room would be my new studio. I fought this idea for a while; I didn't want to change her room. Changing her room would mean that she was not coming back. Changing her room would mean that I was not preserving her memory. Changing her room would mean that I was healing, that I was ready to let a part of her go, and that I was ready to give away her things, and I wasn't ready; at least, I wasn't ready until I painted the walls. Then I knew that I was ready, that the grief work I had done had cracked open a sliver of light and faith, and that I was on the right path. After I painted the walls I knew healing was possible.

Healing: Your Way

When you consider that you may be healing from a devastating loss, you may experience what I did. Sometimes you felt like you were taking two steps forward and one step back. How do early signs of healing show up for you? It may take some time for you to recognize indications of healing, as it did for me. It's ok for you go slow, to not know how to heal, or to not want to heal at first; that may be your way of holding on to your loved one.

It's not helpful for you to place judgment on the ways healing begin to show up for you. You are being shown what healing means for you, and only you can shape a grief journey that supports you in the ways you need to be supported. Ask yourself what that is. What support do you need as you continue, month after month and then year after year, to live in a country not of your choosing? What supports you as you travel further along that road may change after a while, or it may not. The important part is to honor your needs, let your feelings be heard and felt, and allow your unique journey to unfold from your innermost being.

Healing: My Way

My daily practice of making time and space to feel everything I was feeling exactly as it appeared, paved the way to my healing. I was not aware at the time that that is what I was doing. There was a strong pull to lose myself in those feelings.

After I painted the walls, healing came in fits and starts. At first I defined for myself what healing is not. Healing is not getting over losing Leah. It is not getting closure on her death. Healing is not feeling better, or looking for the silver lining—at least, it wasn't in the first weeks, months, and even years after she died. The first time I noticed that I didn't cry for a whole day, I felt so much guilt. I don't remember now how much time had passed. I held on to that guilt like a badge of honor. I didn't want to forget her.

Healing, as it appeared early on, had the quality of being able to breathe deeply again. At first I felt like I was holding my breath, waiting to see what would happen. I was in uncharted territory—the unknown. Once I could breathe again, I could feel even more. I didn't expect that! The part of me that knew explained that this was a part of the journey, and that once we got to a point where we were able to feel more, we are led to that place. I began to see grief as a vast, deep pool filled with feelings and stories. I began to see that I entered this vast pool incrementally, inch by inch, and only to the extent that I could at each given moment. I began to see that I would not be given more to feel until I was ready. In my early healing days, when I was aware of my journey, this gave me great comfort. I would not have to feel the entire mess of feelings all at once; I could wait until I was ready.

It was about this time that I began to get a glimpse of my future work. I would hear, *Someday you will help others through this journey in a way that looks different than you ever imagined.* To be truthful, when I heard that I was both intrigued and terrified. Intrigued, because if I were able to help others, it must be possible for me to reach a point of true healing, where I felt at peace with my journey and could find purpose after losing Leah. I was terrified of the road I would have to travel to get there. I saw people who lost loved one turning around in a year or two to create foundations or events that honored their loved ones. Doing that seemed so foreign to me. Thinking about how to do that and what to do drained my energy and took me back to the depths of my grief. What I came to know is that my journey through my grief is exactly right for me. Yours is exactly right for you. If you are called to create a foundation for your loved one, follow that inspiration. There will be gifts and difficulties along the way, and they will be meticulously designed for your precise journey.

If I am to be honest about healing, Samyama was my lifeline. When I could bring my darkest feelings to my heart, I could enter that pool of grief and feel my feelings. Even that was not a linear, progressive journey. Learning to trust my heart was one of my biggest lessons along the way. What I can tell you is that every time I did bring those feelings to my heart I found grace, or a blessing, every time, without fail. It was that consistent result that eventually led me to trust my heart with all my feelings about losing her: the guilt, the relief, the sadness, and the devastation—all of it.

I have learned that healing is a process. Even as I write this today, my process continues, and I have faith that it will continue for as long as I breathe. I have learned to trust that process, and to allow it to unfold and unravel at its own pace. I am finding my own way, and it doesn't look like anything I ever could have imagined way back when my grief was fresh. Healing continues to mean that I courageously enter my heart with all my feelings so I can perceive that next layer, which reveals its own blessing. Stepping into the practice of walking with others on their grief journeys has brought me to greater depths of the grief pool—depths that I could not have entered any earlier than the moment I did.

I would not have traversed my own grief journey any other way. I have come to love this process of dancing the spiral of my grief. Saying that brings tears to my eyes. The tears never stop; they come whenever a new level of understanding is near. More than ever, I know that the path that Leah and I are on in this lifetime is one of unknown dimensions. I have come to accept and know my own unique way of being in this world, which includes all of me, not only the way that I grieve.

When I first noticed that my daily experience of grief was shifting, I was in denial; I did not want to heal because I didn't know what it meant. I didn't know if it meant I would forget about Leah. If this is your experience, take some time to acknowledge this denial and the feelings that arise. The stages of grief did not visit me in a linear fashion. Each time a stage or feeling came around again it would bring with it new insights, new shifts in feeling, and a different ways of looking at a circumstance. Honor your own spiral of grief; it is exactly what you need for your own journey. When you do sense that healing is on the horizon, feel what it feels like. You will not forget your loved one. All of the ways that you have honored them will make sure that does not happen. You can use some of the same things that helped you with your initial grief, now; write about it, collage; create your own healing ritual.

Stephen Jenkinson, author of *Die Wise* says;

> *"From a young age we see around us that grief is mostly an affliction, a misery that intrudes into the life we deserve, a rupture of the natural order of things, a trauma that we need coping and management and five stages and twelve steps to get over.*
>
> *Here's the revolution: What if grief is a skill, in the same way that love is a skill, something that must be learned and cultivated and taught? What if grief is the natural order of things, a way of loving life anyway? Grief and the love of life are twins, natural human skills that can be learned first by being on the receiving end and feeling worthy of them, later by practicing them when you run short of understanding. In a time like ours, grieving is a subversive act."*

Things To Try:

Each person's healing journey is as unique as your grief. It's helpful to consider what healing means for you.

1. Take some time to consider what healing means to you. How does it show up in your life? What signs appear? Keep track of these signs, even if you're not sure if they indicate healing.

2. How can you develop grief as a skill in your life?

3. When you read that grief is a skill, what does that bring up for you?

QUESTIONS FOR YOUR JOURNAL:

- What does looking at grief as a skill mean to you?
- How do you know you are healing?
- What is healing not for you?
- What will you have to surrender or give up to begin to heal?
- What will you gain?
- What does healing feel like in your body?
- What practices help you to process your feelings as you are healing?
- How can you honor your loved one?

"When you get the choice to sit it out or dance,
I hope you dance"

—Leeann Womack

CHAPTER 8
Grief as Initiation

Alone in the Darkness

I was alone in the darkness as I drove to work. I dreaded this time every morning—alone with my thoughts, no one to see the tears flowing steadily, all the way to work. I had recently begun to receive songs from Leah as a way to communicate with me. A week or so ago I heard "My Girl" on the radio. Dan and I used to sing it to her as a child, and she used to dance and giggle as we sang. As soon as I heard it I knew she had sent it, and I got chills. I asked her to send me more songs.

That day as I got on the expressway, "I Hope You Dance," by Leeann Womack, began to play. It was the first time I heard it, and not recognizing it, I reached out to switch the channel. I paused for a moment as I heard, "May you never take one single breath for granted." My hand froze before it reached the radio. I listened to the words; it felt like Leah was singing directly into my heart. My tears came freely; in the darkness of the morning I welcomed them, without fear of being found out. I was reminded of what I heard right after Leah died: losing Leah was too high a price to pay to not be true to myself. I have kept that thought close to my heart, not knowing how to attempt to even get back to where I was before Leah left, let alone to continue my inner work of personal growth. I didn't even know what that meant. The words to this song are in my heart now. From the first moment I heard them, I knew they were from Leah. It was her way of reminding me to keep going when I felt hopeless, to continue to claw my way out of the raw devastation.

I sat in the car for a moment to compose myself. I had just pulled into the parking garage at work. I dried my eyes again, gathered up the wad of tissues scattered around me, and took a deep breath as I got out of the car and walked to the trailer that houses my office. As I arrived in my office, I immediately began to cry again, so I closed my door and allowed the tears to continue. Even at this early stage in my grieving process I knew that that trying to stop my tears prematurely didn't work. I was the only one in the trailer at the time, and I felt comfortable taking this time for myself.

I heard the trailer door opening and closing; others were beginning to arrive. I continued to cry. I was thankful that I moved out of the office that I was in the day of Leah's accident, thankful that I don't have to relive that particular memory every day, yet here it was again. I felt the tears beginning to subside, and then the door to my office opened abruptly.

I looked up at the elevator subcontractor through tear-stained eyes, so shocked that he had just burst into my office without knocking that I didn't have any words. I looked at him with wide eyes and an open mouth.

"What the hell!?" he yelled at me. "Why are you crying? I need the elevator machine room opened now!"

I was even more shocked that he was raising his voice to me.

I felt an initial moment of panic. He didn't know my story, I didn't want to tell it to him, and I wanted him to leave so I could sit in the shame of being found crying. I wondered why he didn't ask someone else, someone who didn't have her office door closed. I took a deep breath, and then another, and somehow found my voice.

"Go out and find a superintendent in the building. Ask him." I closed the door again. My voice was surprisingly strong, certainly stronger than I felt. I took another deep breath and realized that he had completely disregarded my boundaries. My door was closed! My shame turned to disbelief and incredulity that someone would ignore my closed door and then be upset when he found me crying inside. I realized that my crying had made him uncomfortable and he had lashed out to hide it. I took another deep breath, trying to calm the myriad feelings coursing through my body. My shame gave way to an acknowledgement that I took a stand for my needs and for myself. I breathed that knowledge into my body, letting it slowly infiltrate my entire being, relaxing as I did. I held my head up high, no longer feeling shame and no longer wanting to hide in my office to avoid seeing the elevator subcontractor. I had a meeting with him later that day. I knew that I would attend the meeting without needing to explain anything to him—without needing to diminish my actions. The wisdom of this newfound knowledge was infused through my entire body. My tears dried. I opened the door to my office and began my day.

Ordinary Time

After the funeral or memorial service is over your friends will continue to think about you and help you out when they can, but they are back at their everyday lives, while your life remains changed. After a certain amount of time you realize that your loved one is not coming back, and that you need to continue on with your life. It is likely that the pain you carry with you is not always visible to others around you. I used to wonder if people could see my pain in line at the grocery store. There is no set amount of time that this is likely to happen. It can come and go in waves, with all the feelings and stages of grief swirling around you in seemingly random patterns. Maybe you aren't crying every day and you feel guilty about it. Or you find yourself laughing and you stop yourself because you are supposed to be sad. You may be reluctant to talk about your feelings to some people because you think they will expect you to be further along your healing path.

Learning how to navigate the ordinary-ness of your grief journey can be just as exhausting as early grief. For one thing, you are beginning to realize the finality of losing a loved one. Month after month and then year after year, they are still not there. It was in the midst of this ordinary grief that my journey morphed into initiation. Perhaps yours will, too.

Recognition

Even in my altered state I recognized that some things were shifting for me. The situation of navigating my daughter's death was compelling me to take care of myself in a new way. All along the way there were moments that suggested to me that I was growing, as I took on the initiation of life after Leah.

The situation with the subcontractor was not the first time I thought of my grief process as an initiation, but it was one of the first times I recognized that the way I responded to the situation had changed the way I felt afterwards. In the past I may have just gotten up and shut the door without saying anything to the person barging in on me, and I would have felt shame and guilt for not standing up for myself, or for letting someone else see a part of myself that I did not want them to see. Or, I might have tried to explain to him why he found me crying, needing to make him understand in order for me to feel better myself. I was beginning to see that an initiation has the power to deconstruct and unravel all of the old wounds and parts of myself that needed to be healed. By meeting the feelings of my daughter's death, I was being shown ways to take a stand for myself. I was discovering parts of myself that were strong and resilient, parts of myself that I knew were there. Parts of myself that I never had the courage to bring forward. Grieving for my daughter was changing the way I interacted in the world and the way I engaged with those around me. Grieving for my daughter was changing me. I began to feel like my initiation was alchemy.

Initiation has several meanings. It is both a rite of passage from one stage of life to another, and the beginning of something. I began to experience it as the beginning of moving from one stage of life to another; life before Leah died, and after she died. Her death was the event that started the initiation, but I chose to enter it. That act alone set my course even though the course was unknown. I took a stand to try to make meaning out of an event that made no sense. I entered unknown territory without any idea of what I would find.

Alchemy is defined as the process of transforming something common into something special in an inexplicable or mysterious way. In medieval times, it was a chemical and speculative science that aimed to turn base metals into gold.

What do I mean when I say that alchemy happens in the initiation? As I continued to live year after year without Leah's physical presence in my life, and met the feelings that arose in each moment, some incredible shifts began to happen. I could not make peace with Leah's death by trying to figure it out in my head. No amount of turning it this way and that way could help me make sense of why it happened, or that it did happen. When I held the feelings in my heart in the practice of Samyama, and allowed the feelings to be there as they appeared, I learned to allow them to be there without any attachment. I didn't know how they would be resolved, or if they would be resolved, or what the outcome would even look like. The more I surrendered to this practice, the more I trusted the unknown, and the alchemy began to happen. The raw devastation turned to gold—the gold of understanding.

It was a slow process; all of the constructs I had learned had to be deconstructed. I began to understand that I could find purpose in life after Leah. Did I want it? *No,* screamed my head. *I can't accept this. I want my daughter back.* In those moments I returned to my heart and trusted that my heart could hold all the feelings as they were. I discovered peace in those moments.

I learned that it's not the goal to remain in my heart everyday, all the time. It is the return to the heart that creates the alchemy.

As the months continued, I no longer defined myself as grieving for my daughter. The path through my grief was bringing me into the light. I know that now. I did not want to know it for a long, long time. It is not something that I understand; it is something I know in my heart. It is here without emotion, true to the way my intuition shows up for me. I feel Leah's presence in all of this; I wonder if she has come to understand without question that this path we are on together is necessary for each of us. Walking the path through the unknown has become more comfortable and familiar as I face the mystery.

Following my intuition led me to Samyama. It became my path through my grief and led to my initiation. My initiation too began to take the shape of a spiral. Each time I returned to a feeling while traveling the spiral I gained new insights because I was in a different place, a new moment. The same feeling could elicit new understanding by virtue of meeting each one in the present moment. The deeper I traveled the spiral of my initiation, the more my decisions and choices took on the quality of alchemy. One of those decisions was to enter the Samyama Apprenticeship and become certified as a Samyama Practitioner. As I traveled that journey, most of the clients who came to me were grief clients. At that time I was not asking for grief clients. The universe was already giving me a glimpse of my future path.

Through my initiatory journey, I began to realize that I had a unique perspective that could help others who were also on their own grief journeys. I imagined what this would look like. My journey tempered me and tested me many times. My writing began to take on new meaning. It would take a while before I recognized that this was my path. I was excavating a self that I could only glimpse from afar before this journey began. The alchemy of the initiation brought me to the fullness of my authentic self.

A few weeks after I first heard "I Hope You Dance," I intuitively received a message from Leah: "Thank you for being who you are, so that I could be who I am." I continued to be utterly in awe of the journey I was on. As soon as I surrendered to a perception or the physical longing of missing my daughter, I was given an incredible insight.

Acknowledging your Own Initiation

Your initiation can help you to excavate your true purpose in this world, too. If the work you are doing does not align with the discoveries you are making as you travel your grief journey, you can discover the work you are meant to do in this world in the way you are meant to do it.

How will you know you are ready for your initiation? What are some of the things you notice about your life now that you didn't notice before your loss?

You may already be in an initiation and not realize it. You can also intentionally enter into an initiation. Take some time to notice how you are feeling. There may some softening around your heart when you think about your loved one. You may feel like you are healing, and you may now be feeling like you want to heal. Take a look at where you are today, and where you were in the early days of your loss. Is there a difference? A shifting of your feelings? How do you measure progress? It is not measured by anyone else's rules or guidelines.

You can enter an initiation at any point in your life. You may think you have to be at a certain point in you life before you take on an initiation. The opposite is true. Your initiation will inform your journey. The invitation to enter it where you are now is an opportunity waiting for you to say, "Yes."

For a long time I thought that I was not evolved enough for the work of the Temple of the Sacred Feminine. The fear of not being good enough held me back. When Leah died, there was a fearlessness that took over. There was a sense of importance, and my intuition was just developed enough at that point to step into the unknown. Leah's death let me know that I was already living in the unknown; I was just unaware. To knowingly step into the unknown territory of an initiation can be frightening. It can also save your life, like it did mine.

I have come to know that my grief journey has led me to the full expression of who I am. I surrendered parts of myself that no longer served me. My life has been deconstructed and reconstructed several times, it seems. It took a long time for me to fully accept that my work in the world is to walk with others on their grief journeys and help them step into a full expression of who they are and how they show up in the world. When I did accept my role, I felt like myself—the self I had been seeking all my life. If you are ready to walk this journey for yourself, find someone to facilitate your journey. All you need is the willingness to enter.

Things to Try:

Initiation may be a new way to look at your grief journey.

1. Make a collage to represent your initiation. How can you represent alchemy in your collage?

2. Take some time to consider if there parts of yourself that you will have to surrender as you move through your grief journey. How do you know?

3. Notice if you react or respond to the things people say to you about your grief. What is the difference between reacting and responding? What difference does it make in your journey?

QUESTIONS FOR YOUR JOURNAL:

🪶 What does initiation mean for you?

🪶 How will you know you are ready for your initiation?

🪶 Do you feel like there is some softening around your heart when you think about your loved one?

🪶 Do you feel like you are healing? How do you know?

🪶 Do you feel like you have made progress?

🪶 How do you measure progress? It is not measured by anyone else's rules or guidelines.

🪶 Are you ready to discover a new meaning to your grief?

🪶 Are you ready to discover the gifts of your grief journey?

My soul longs to know its Truth. And when I ask myself how I live now that
Leah is gone;
My soul screams out, "Feel the pain! Be true to me!"
And when I am the joy cannot be contained.
I am devastated by pain and exploding with joy.
The very essence of my spirit
Knows what my ego refuses to see.
My soul expands with the knowledge of Truth.
Pure joy in the same space as utter devastation.

—From My Journal, 11/2003

CHAPTER 9
Staying and Leaving

Leaving my Job

I had 11 more days to work before leaving my career of almost 20 years. It was more than a job; it had been my training ground, in so many ways, for what was coming next. This part of my career took me from a timid version of myself, to a woman who is confident and able to stand up to even the wiliest subcontractor. I am many offices and jobsites away from the office I sat in on the day my reality changed, almost 13 years ago. I sat in my office and looked through the box filled with my personal items, the things that made my office my own. It holds pictures of my family, a shell I picked up at the beach to remind me to listen, tea, a candle that I burned when I needed additional centering, usually after 4 PM most days. There were a few of things Leah's too: a rock she painted for me, a drawing. Next to that box were things I'd leave behind: my hardhat and safety vest, my office supplies, marked-up drawings from the buildings that are getting ready to be turned over. There's a bright orange raincoat and overalls hanging on the back of my door that make me smile as I remembered who gave them to me.

All of a sudden, tears racked my body. I was unable to stop, and it surprised me. I had been planning my departure for some time, and many people knew about it. Some were surprised that I was still doing my job as if I wasn't leaving. I told them that as long as I was there, I was committed to my daily responsibilities. I thought that all my preparation laid the groundwork for me to leave. If that was the case, why was I crying? I was reminded, once again, that grief doesn't wait for a convenient time to show up. It is meticulous in its task. It doesn't wait for a convenient time to arrive. No—true to its nature, it shows up at precisely the right time; it shows up at the time that will do the most good, the time that will offer the most insight and integration. So I let the tears flow as I remembered everyone I had worked with through the years: the person who hired me, the first project I was on, everyone who had crossed my path during my time there. I said a silent thank you to each and every one of them, grateful for the lessons each one brought to me. I was grateful, too, for the way they cared for us when Leah died—the hospital visits, the food, the breakfast on the day of her funeral, the calls for lunch and dinner that coaxed us back to life when we all we wanted to do was stay in our cocoon of pain. My crying subsided; the last tears silently rolled down my cheeks. I looked at the mound of tissues on my desk and took a deep breath. The sadness of a few minutes ago was ebbing; I felt the clarity of my next chapter beckoning me. I should've been used to the way grief works by then. I should've known to expect the unexpected, I should've... and then I stopped, as I heard myself say, "should've." There is no "should," no way to anticipate the onslaught of grief.

After the tears stopped, I took a sip of water and continued to reflect on my time here and what was coming next. I thought that my preparation to move to what is next would shield me from grieving. I thought that since I knew instinctively that my next chapter was a result of the work I had done through the initiation of Leah's death, it would guarantee that I would joyfully skip down the path to the fulfillment of my dreams. And it would, but not before I honored where I was coming from, and gave myself enough time in between where I was and where I was going to complete the processing of my feelings. Yes, I would have to grieve my career before I could joyfully skip down that path.

I wish I could tell you that the day I left my job, I wholeheartedly took on my work to support others on their grief journeys. I had a few more twists and turns before that happened. There were a few detours on that path before I reached where I thought I was going. All of the perceived detours were also necessary preparation. I took several trainings, one of them as an Eating Psychology Coach. I worked with a business coach, and began integrating my training into my life, and thought I had arrived in the future of my dreams. And then I learned the meaning of this Rumi quote: "A thousand half-loves must be forsaken to take one whole heart home."

In one of my coaching calls, when I was talking about the direction of my Eating Psychology business, Nourished Body, Wild Heart, a participant asked me a question. She wanted to know if I was sure of the direction I was headed.

She wondered if I was more suited to grief work, given the depth of my sharing about my initiation. I was suitably horrified. I couldn't sleep. I was shaken to my core. If I had been on the wrong path, I had wasted a lot of money and time. I convinced myself that I could make it work the way I was going, but there remained an uneasy feeling in my gut. My body was beginning to inform me that I was not in fact on the right path. My prayer was to trust that I would be shown the right way.

Soon after this, I attended a retreat at the Joyful Journey Hot Springs in Colorado with the same coaching group. The retreat provided for wonderful connection with the women in the group, during yoga, feminine embodiment work, sharing of good food, breaks in the hot springs, and individual coaching sessions with the facilitators.

I started a novena, a nine-day prayer ritual the week before the retreat. I planned it this way so that the ninth day would coincide with the last day of the retreat. My intention for the novena was, " I am ready and willing to step fully into my work. I ask for clarity to unapologetically stand in my Truth to serve the world in alignment with Divine Intent." I spent time each day sitting in prayer with my intent, and writing about my process.

When it was my turn for my turn for individual coaching, I was feeling a deep connection with all of the other women. My time in the chair came last, after some amazing work by my sister business priestesses. I watched major breakthroughs and shifts in their business plans. I was in awe of the deep work we were doing.

I wondered what would happen when it was my turn. I didn't think I would have any breakthroughs. As I sat in the chair and began describing my business, I also shared one of my revelations from day two or three of my novena: that the initiation of Leah's death birthed me to do the work I was called to do in the world, and that a life of joy is possible even after such a devastating life event. I was then asked, point blank, "Why are you not helping people navigate their grief journeys and showing them the possibilities of a joyful life?"

I gulped. A part of me said, "But what about all I have done to get the business I was pursuing, Nourished Body, Wild Heart, launched?" Another part of me said, "Finally!"

The leaders of the group continued to skillfully guide me with questions to excavate my true calling. I felt like I was in the company of loving midwives. As I got closer and closer to stepping fully into work to support others on their grief journeys, I felt my body aligning with my purpose. I felt the energy of this work rising from my core. I remembered all the times since Leah died that I said I was going to help others recover a life of joy after losing a loved one. And finally, I stepped fully and unapologetically into my work to walk with those on their grief journeys, and Being With Grief was born.

I was finally able to hear my authentic voice, and I could no longer ignore it. The question I was asked a few weeks before the retreat cracked the shell of the seed of my greatest calling. The laser question at the retreat cultivated the seed, allowing my heart to bloom, finally.

Knowing the Signs

How will you know when your present life no longer aligns with your highest vision for yourself? Here are some places to start.

Feeling Stuck

We often feel stuck, or like we are in a rut, shortly before we are ready for a breakthrough. We may stay here longer than necessary because it feels safer, and it is known. When we think of moving from a stuck place, we often face more fear and worry about what it will take to move through the stuck feelings. When these feelings intensify, it is time to take notice of them; they are intensifying to get your attention.

Feeling Chaos

Does your life feel chaotic, like everything is spinning out of control faster and faster? Take some time to consciously slow down. Notice what happens when you do. Often, more feelings will begin to arise. When we are too busy and not allowing ourselves time to feel, our feelings need to spin out of control to get our attention. When you give your feelings the attention they deserve, they quiet down a little; they let you know what is needed. You may find out things you are now ready to know.

Whispering from your Intuition

When you slow down, you give your intuition space to speak. You may begin to receive insights that were slow to come when you were filling every minute with activity. As you slow down, are you feeling a sense that something is not right, or that there is something more to your life? Maybe you have been on your grief journey for a while. You have begun to recognize a shift in your life; things don't seem to fit any longer. Your priorities have changed.

Your Feelings

Honor your feelings. Everyone has their own way of processing feelings, and feelings about grief are no different. If you feel sad, let yourself cry. Maybe you are feeling irritated with those around you. You want them to change. This is another big clue that you are ready to move to new ground and it's time to change your way of thinking. Write about your feelings. Sometimes capturing your feelings in your journal can give you some perspective.

Dreams

As I prepared to step into the fullness of my being, my dreamtime became very active, helping in the preparation. In one dream I was in the conference room at my present job, with all the people from that job as well as people from the work I would be stepping into. I asked where I could find my new place to work, and someone told me it was far away from here, through the forest; I should follow the lights. I went out and found myself in a forest. It was dark, and all of the trees had white lights on them. It was foggy, and though I began running, I did not trip or fall in the darkness. As I ran, I saw a city lit up across a bridge—a long, swinging bridge across a huge abyss. It also had lights on it. I ran across the bridge without hesitation, something I would not have done in real life. I was fearless as I approached the lights in the city. I woke up just before I got there.

In another dream, a few nights later, I was in a complex configuration of places, and getting from place to place was again difficult. This was a familiar landscape from past dreams. At one point in the dream I was told the world was ending, but I did not believe it. I stayed calm while others around me did not. Just before I woke up, I was in a crowded room with a woman who set a timer to 2 hours, 10 minutes; this, she said, was when the world would probably end. I remained calm and wordlessly communicated to Dan that it would not happen for us. These dreams made it clear to me that I was ready to enter my new life.

I often dream that I am pregnant, or giving birth, as I am working on a new project. That was especially true as I was writing this book.

Time

It's not time itself that shifts your grief process, but rather what you do with that time. You may begin referring to your time as Before your Loss and After your Loss. This is the in-between time. What you do with the time in between the life you left and the one you are headed towards, is important. When you lose a loved one or a job, end a relationship, or your life takes some other unexpected turn, name it as grief, as loss, or as something or someone you will miss. Take some time to feel the feelings that this loss evokes. No one knows how long it will take you to shift your feelings—not even you. By diligently attending to your feelings and your process, one day you will feel a shift, receive a new insight or awareness, and see things differently. Allow yourself to acknowledge these new insights when they come.

Surrender or Letting Go

Be open to surrender and let go when it feels right to do so. Hanging on to things from our past that no longer serve us, keeps us from being in the present moment. When we don't honor our own grieving processes we tend to hold onto things, hoping our experience will change and things will go back to being the way they were.

Acknowledging that you are stuck, or ready to move from a place that no longer serves you, is the first step to actually moving forward. Knowing when to ask for help is important, too. Sometimes I would go around and around with myself about the importance of listening to inner guidance or seeking support. What I know is that both are necessary. Learning how to listen to your own inner guidance and wisdom goes hand-in-hand with looking to an expert to assist with learning a new skill, do inner soul work, get health, life, or business coaching, or even for technical assistance with your computer. What I have discovered is that my inner guidance will let me know the right coach or mentor to work with at the right time.

One of my mentors says, "You're not ready until you're ready." When you are in touch with your intuition and your inner wisdom, the right person or opportunity will always show up at precisely the right time.

Things to Try:

Making a change can be daunting. Knowing your own signposts can be helpful.

1. Take notice of your dreams. Keep a note pad by your bed and record them as soon as you wake up. What can you notice from your dreams that are indicating a change? Is there a reoccurring theme in your dreams? What is ready to be born in your life now?

2. Make a list of all of the things that make you feel safe. Has it changed from the first list you made? You can continue to refine this list. Look at it often to check in with yourself to see if you are feeling safe.

3. If you are longing for a change and you aren't sure how to affect a change, ask for guidance. In Samyama we learn how to drop questions

in our heart without attachment to what shows up or how it looks. Try that for yourself when you aren't sure of what's next.

4. Consciously slow down. Try it with everything you do: bathing, brushing your teethe, eating, dressing. Take deep breaths as you move slowly through your day. Notice the difference when you take things slowly.

QUESTIONS FOR YOUR JOURNAL:

🦢 What are some ways you can surrender what no longer serves you?

🦢 How do you know you are ready to surrender old stuff?

🦢 How might you honor your feelings in a way that feels true to who you are?

🦢 Do you find yourself wishing things were different than they are? Write about that.

🦢 What feelings come up when you contemplate breaking out of the rut you are in?

"It's not about feeling better, it's about getting better at feeling."

—**Michael Brown**, *The Presence Process*

CHAPTER 10

Grief is Not Contagious

Owning Your Own Feelings

All things considered, most people are afraid of grief; they don't want to talk about it, or think about it, or see how it touches their lives. In the days after my daughter's death, I felt like my very presence could clear a grocery store, or give us an entire church pew to ourselves. I felt like when some people recognized that I was the woman whose daughter died, they went out of their way to avoid me so they didn't have to talk to me. Not knowing what to say and not wanting to say something hurtful created a distance between me and many people in our community. Being unable to find a connection to bridge the chasm that was created when Leah died, they stayed away. I understood that seeing me made them uncomfortable. Seeing me reminded them that they, too, could have an experience like mine, and that was too hard to think about. I understood that, too. I felt their eyes averting as they thought, "There's the woman whose daughter died." I tried to stand tall and show them I was strong, but the tears always came, and I felt the waves of discomfort emanating from their beings. I wanted to tell them that they couldn't catch grief from talking to me, or from getting too close to me. I wanted to tell them that they couldn't keep their children safer if they refused to engage with a grieving mother. I wanted to tell them that because I lost my daughter, there was no correlation to them losing their child. I wanted to tell them that grief is not contagious.

Remembrance Gathering

I sat waiting for our guests to arrive. I was filled with trepidation. The invitation was met with many questions from our friends and Leah's friends.

"What are you going to do?"

"What should I expect?"

"What time is it again?"

"It's at your house?"

"I'm not sure what to expect. Can you tell me again?"

"I can't come, I'm busy that day. When is it again? Yes, I'm busy."

As I waited, I wondered if anyone would come. Would the fear of the unknown keep them away, like it kept some people from talking to us at church or the grocery store? As I waited, I remembered how it felt to walk into a room where everyone sees me and no one acknowledges me. Would today be similar? Would our friends and Leah's friends stay away today to avoid facing their feelings of fear? Would they come, but then dash off when it got too uncomfortable for them to be here? It had been only six months since Leah's death, on what would have been her 18th birthday. I thought of the irony of that. Leah could not wait for her 18th birthday. It was a milestone that represented liberation to her; she was just about ready to leave home and begin exploring the world for herself. She had looked forward to a birthday party.

Instead of an 18th birthday party we are having a Remembrance Gathering. It is a get-together of those who loved her, to remember her and her light in our lives. I looked up to see our dear friend who was facilitating the Remembrance Gathering arriving. She had been a constant in my life since Leah died; she smiled at me and hugged me as she walked up to our door. No words were exchanged, yet I feel calmer. We went inside and I showed her where we would be, and she began her own preparations. The doorbell rang, and I answered it to let in some friends, and invited them to go downstairs where Dan and Peter got them settled. The doorbell rang again. I opened the door and saw cars lining up and down both sides of the street, and more parking a few houses away. Leah's friends and ours were streaming into our house, and I wondered if we would have enough room.

When it was time for us to begin, and our friend asked everyone to sit comfortably as she invited everyone to be present.

"Today we gather to remember and celebrate Leah. Nancy, Dan, and Peter have invited all of you here today to reflect and share memories of her."

As I listened to her words, I looked around the room. Our friends and work colleagues, Leah's friends, Peter's friends. All together, more than forty people were gathered. None of them knew what to expect, yet all of them were willing to be here. I took a deep breath, and returned to the instructions for the day. Pieces of paper were passed out so we could write our prayers for Leah. We lined up to get a piece of red cloth, a pinch of tobacco, and a piece of string. Everyone placed their prayer and the tobacco into the red fabric and tied it with the string to make a pouch. Music played as we worked. We went outside to form a circle on our patio near three large pine trees. I looked around at all of the faces. Many were still not sure what to expect, yet they were all there.

I found my voice. "Thank you all for being here today. Our prayer bundles are made in the custom of the Piscataway Indian tradition of honoring their dead. The Piscataway believe that the messages in the bundles are carried to their loved ones on the wind. We will now place our prayer bundles on the tree. When you place your bundle, I invite you to share a story or memory of Leah, if you would like."

I took my place in the circle as the first person stepped forward to hang her prayer bundle and share a thought about Leah.

Leah's friend Corrine remembered,

"When Leah died I gained a whole new perspective on life. Although Leah's death showed me some of the hardships of life, she more importantly taught me to live life day to day, and to not live for the past or the future. Leah lived life to its fullest, and she shared her enthusiasm for life with everyone she encountered. Although I was only in her life for a few short months, I was lucky enough to experience Leah's contagious enthusiasm and spark for life. I have had several dreams about Leah since her death, and I feel like she has spoken to me through the dreams. I thank God for allowing me to become so close with Leah, even though we were not friends for very long. We shared secrets, memories, fun times, and hard times, and those times will always be treasured. Leah Loeffler will forever hold a very influential piece of my heart, and I thank you for helping me keep that part alive."

Another friend shared,

"I cherish my memories of Leah. I will always remember our times spent together, and the fun we had. Leah's ability to reach people was amazing. She left a lasting impression on anyone she met. She never let me touch her hair though, that was her area of expertise. We loved acting goofy. Sometimes we would make up funny dances and just laugh at ourselves. I loved it when Leah got excited and let out her little squeals. Remembering Leah puts a smile on my face and a tear in my eye. She was an unforgettable person, and I am blessed to have been so close to her."

I was in awe as person after person stepped forward to share their stories. We laughed and we cried. We remembered, and we were there for each other. When the tree was regaled with red bundles, I described our next activity.

"When we go back inside, we will write a collaborative poem for Leah. Each person will write one line, and will see only the line before their line. After you write your line, fold over the page so that the next person will see only your line."

We headed back inside; I put on music and passed out the pages. Everyone wrote his or her line of the poem. After we were done, we headed back outside in our circle and read the poem, while we each held a candle. I looked around again. My heart was full. I could not express what I was feeling, yet I knew that what had just occurred would play a big part in the grief journeys of everyone in attendance.

When we were done, we invited everyone into the house for food. We gathered some of Leah's favorite foods to share. The mood had changed completely.

"We didn't know what to expect, but it wasn't this."

"How did you think of doing something like this?"

"You are so brave."

"I will remember this for a long time."

"I really didn't want to come, but I'm glad I did."

"Thank you."

On and on, I listened to the comments. I was numb—from grief, from gratitude, from showing people a different way to do things. Although I didn't realize it yet, my ministry had begun.

Grief Changes Us

Today, when I talk about grief, I have experience to draw from. I understand that grief is difficult to talk about. Grief brings us face to face with parts of ourselves that we don't want to see—parts of ourselves that we think we are better off burying as deep as we can. I probably thought that, too, before I was dragged through my own grief. Grief that stays underground festers. Grief that is not allowed to see the light of day seeps into the marrow of our bones. It hides until it can no longer contain itself, and then it shows up in unrecognizable ways. It morphs into all of our accumulative losses. It is big and ugly and fuels our fear. This is the grief that I want to untangle. I was plopped right in the middle of this thing called grief. I wanted to dissect it, to pull it apart by its seams, to see what it was made of, to try to make sense of what seemed so senseless to me.

Today I know that grief is not contagious. What is the unseen force that keeps people from wanting to engage grief, to avoid those who are grieving? From my experience there are several reasons.

The first is the drive to stay in a comfortable place, if you talk to the person who lost her daughter, you will be forced to look at her pain, you may even start to think about the possibility of something like that happening to you. You can't go there, so you retreat.

Talking with someone who has lost a loved one forces us to consider a loss so immense that we feel physically ill. If we avoid those who are grieving, maybe we can avoid grief visiting our life and the lives of those we love.

We also like to fix things. On the quest to make things better, we want to fix the griever's life, and we can't. No one can.

I'd venture to suggest that someone who reacts in these ways is not feeling comfortable, either. Our intentions are good; we want to help, we just don't often know how.

That makes us uncomfortable. I'd like to propose that one way to be with a griever is to become more adept at feeling our feelings, and letting others feel theirs; there is a way for each of us to let others have uncomfortable feelings, and a way for them to do the same for us when the time comes. When we name our feelings, we become willing to own them.

I see grief these days as a tangle of many different feelings and emotions, wrapped around the stories that hold its form. It is almost like another entity that we live with until we begin to loosen the knots of emotions, so we can feel the feelings that allow the stories to unravel and reveal their precious gifts.

What if we could begin to see the value of meeting our grief head-on rather than trying to avoid it? What if talking about grief was as natural as talking about the weather? What if a mother who lost her daughter could be held by the other mothers in the neighborhood, in a rite of passage much like childbirth, or celebrations of birthdays, or weddings or other milestones? What if sadness was honored and allowed the same way we welcome joy and happiness? And yet joy and happiness seems so elusive, if we are to believe the headlines that tell us how to search for happiness, or find joy. What if the way to find happiness and joy is by embracing sadness and pain? What if there were no good and bad feelings, or positive or negative emotions? What if all feelings and emotions are merely here to be felt and embraced as they are, without attachment to what we think we should or shouldn't do with them?

This has been my journey. Denying it, feeling it, not wanting to feel it, and being willing to feel it. Back and forth and over all the possible ways to get rid of grief, to meet it, to go around it, and to let it pass through me until I could no longer deny its presence or its power to transform me.

If we wait until we experience a tragic loss to begin feeling our feelings as they are, and to allow others to witness those feelings, then it will take longer to get to the place of feeling comfortable with our feelings. What if we start now, making a commitment to ourselves to begin feeling our feelings exactly as they are, without trying to change them, deny them, or internalize them? Would we be better equipped to feel the really difficult ones when we experience a loss? I'd like to think we would.

Things to Try:

Grief can be difficult and challenges us with every step. It is not, however, contagious, and our feelings can lead us through the difficult times.

1. Consider planning a celebration that honors your loved one on a special milestone. It could be a birthday or other special day for you and your family. Create a ritual or celebration that is meaningful to you.

2. How can you start being better at feeling your feelings now? What would have to change?

3. How do you feel when you don't allow your feelings to come up—when you repress them? What happens when you do that?

QUESTIONS FOR YOUR JOURNAL:

- What has grief propelled you to do now, that you would not have done prior to your loss?

- Have you felt excluded from your friends' lives since your loss?

- What difference would it make in your life if grief was discussed freely and not avoided or pushed away?

- When someone is able to connect with you in your grief, how do you feel?

The light grows insistent; I cannot deny it any more than I can deny death, so
I squint in the sunlight, will I get burned?
But I have stood in the fire; I am tempered like steel.
Do I have courage to face the brilliance, to accept another death?
I want to scream NO, but I know it's a lie.
I stand at the edge of nothingness, eyes closed, illuminated.
I dive into the abyss, dying another death,
how many more must I endure?

—From My Journal, 4/2003

CHAPTER 11
Blessing and Grace

Divine Illumination

Depending on the religious or spiritual tradition you follow, the word "blessing" or the word "grace" may already hold unique definitions for you. Maybe they do, or maybe they don't; let me tell you what I mean by blessing and grace. I've come to see a direct connection between my ability to be with my feelings that arise from each facet of my grief journey and blessings and grace. A blessing can be a kind word from a friend, a prayer of protection, or a reminder from a friend of Leah's of her continued impact on his or her life. Grace is divine assistance. Grace is part of the alchemy, the unexplained events that bring a sense of wonder to our lives. And, for me, grace grants a temporary reprieve from the pain of missing my daughter. Blessings and grace are gifts.

Unexpected Blessings

The day was April 28th. It was Leah's birthday, another birthday without her. That day is hard for me, no matter the year. I can't celebrate my daughter growing another year older. I can celebrate, but I celebrate without her. I have ice cream in her memory because she loved—no, LOVED ice cream. One of her best jobs was working at an ice cream stand. I can have her favorite dinner, in her honor. I can remind myself how old she would have been on this birthday, and wonder what she would have been like at 21, 25, or 30. Would she still like ice cream? Probably. Would her favorite flavor still be mint chocolate chip? All these things I have to wonder. Leah's birthday starts what I used to call the first triple whammy of the year: her birthday, Mother's Day, and my birthday in mid-June. The second triple whammy is the anniversary of her death, Thanksgiving and Christmas. I allowed myself to feel the emptiness of missing her, of not being able to give her a physical hug on her birthday. The physical missing is beyond what I had imagined it could ever be.

This particular year Dan and I planned to go to an overlook we often visited with Leah, up the mountain. We noticed that we were low on gas, so we pulled into a gas station, one that we rarely used. Dan got out to pump the gas and I looked over at a car that had just pulled in. It was one of Leah's teachers, her favorite. I got out of the car. She saw me and got out as well. We hugged; tears came to both of our eyes. She told me a story about how knowing Leah has changed her life, about some decisions she made since Leah's death because life is so short. I had not seen her since Leah's remembrance gathering, on this same day, her birthday, several years ago. We talked for a little while longer, hugged again and we both went our own ways. As we drove up to the overlook, Dan and I talked about the gift of seeing Leah's beloved teacher, and I was grateful for this gift in the midst of my sadness.

Another year, again in the spring, maybe closer to Mother's Day, I had been missing Leah a lot. It's funny how often I say that, as if I go through periods of not missing her as much and then all of a sudden I miss her more. I always miss her. I think that what happens is that I see or hear something that reminds me of her, or a milestone day approaches and I associate a certain memory with her, and the missing seems more intense. Or sometimes when I am missing her achingly, I have a sense that she is nearby and missing me, too.

In the midst of this extra missing of her I went to check the mail. In the mailbox I found a lilac. Another blessing! Lilacs are one of my favorite flowers, and they didn't grow where we were living at the time, or at least not very well. I had a small lilac bush that bloomed occasionally at best, and the blooms were very small. This was a full, lush bloom like the one I had outside my bedroom window as a girl. I knew there were no lilac bushes like this in our neighborhood, but I walked down our road, and then a few more, to look for a bush. I didn't find one. I knew I wouldn't. So, how did it get there? In that moment it didn't matter. It was there. It was another indication of the blessings and grace that show up in my life when I allow my feelings to be there as they are in each moment.

Another time, close to her birthday, every time I got in my car the dome light would be on, and the battery not dead. I made sure the light was not on when I got out of the car, and sure enough the next morning the light would be on again. This went on for a period of about six weeks. By the end of the first week I was triple-checking that the light was turned off when I got home from work. Each morning I could almost hear Leah's gleeful laugh as I got into the car and discovered, once again, that the light was on. It was as if she was telling me, "Lighten up, mom!" something she told me often while she was here.

Seemingly synchronistic events would occur near Leah's or my birthday, and other milestone days. It was like magic, or miracles. There is no other way to explain it. My feelings were always stronger around milestone days. Association with time of year, including the weather, songs, food, or other physical reminders of Leah's absence could bring me back into the pool of grief. When I allowed myself to feel those feelings, I began to notice that there was a connection between feeling difficult feelings and receiving blessings and grace. The physicality of missing her was like an ache that wouldn't go away.

Often the blessing and grace would appear in the form of something physical. I could hold and smell the fragrance of the lilac. I received a hug from Leah's teacher. I began to look forward to the blessings as precious gifts. There was often nothing to explain how or why what happened could have taken place.

When I first began seeing the correlation between fully feeling my feelings and receiving something in return, I could only think of them as blessings and grace—gifts. Thinking of receiving a gift when I was grieving my daughter seemed wrong somehow. As a mother whose daughter died, I no longer had the right to feel joy, or live a life with meaning. My life as I knew it was over, and if anyone would have suggested that I would not only have a meaningful life again, but also find a way to thrive, I wouldn't have believed them. It was a very slow road for me—grappling for understanding, clawing my way out of my ruined life.

It was the constant reminder that losing my daughter was too high a price to pay to not be myself, that kept me going when I reached low points along the way. Seeing the blessings and grace as gifts was one of the first steps to finding meaning again in my life. Those same things—seeing Leah's teacher, finding a lilac in my mailbox—had completely different meanings than they would have without the loss of my daughter.

I began to recognize that Leah and I still had a relationship, and that she was still a part of my life. The form of our relationship had changed, but I began to be willing to know her as she had become. I began to bring her into my heart and hold her there. I began to see the power in the blessing and grace that appears when I have the courage to bring the fullness of my feelings to my heart to feel their pain. I began to go much deeper into Samyama as my practice, knowing that there I could receive the relief I longed for. I learned that I could trust my heart. I began bringing my pain from loss to my heart as soon as I felt it, instead of prolonging the suffering by letting my head try to come up with what I "should have" done. When I went right to my heart with the feelings, I experienced a shift; there was an opening, and a connection to the great heart. The blessings and grace there were immeasurable. After the feelings shifted I could rest in the vastness of my heart.

From this place, receiving gifts took on a new meaning. We are often given gifts, but we don't often receive them fully. We often hold tightly to the way things used to be, or to a life that no longer serves us, or to a story that says we can get back to a way of life that is no longer possible. When we soften our grip on those things by coming into the present moment, we can be open to receive what is in each moment for us—the gift of each moment.

Unexpected Gifts

This image came to me somewhere along my journey. We are given some beautiful seeds to hold, and we are told that these seeds will provide everything we have ever wanted in our life. We hold tight to the seeds, afraid to lose them, keeping our hands clenched in our tight fists. We are determined to hold on to the seeds that will give us the life we want. If we continue to form our hands into tight fists, though, we will never be able to plant the seeds we hold, nor will we be able to open our hands to accept the gifts we are offered.

We do not often think that we can receive gifts from disappointment, loss, or especially grief. We tell ourselves how we should feel, or sometimes others tell us how we should feel. When we allow ourselves to feel what we are feeling, rather than what others expect us to feel, a couple of things may happen. We may be surprised to feel something different than we expected. Consider my client who felt a sense of relief mixed with the sadness after her dog died. The dog had belonged to her mother with whom she had a difficult relationship. Even though she loved the dog, she sometimes felt that the burden of her mother's judgment came with the dog. After the dog died she was surprised to feel some of that burden lifted. If she denied those feelings and listened to others, she may not have received the gift of that lightened burden.

These gifts can come in many forms. They can be physical manifestations, like the lilac or the hug I received. Or they can be lessons or realizations about your situation that you were unable to see even the day before. The gifts or lessons we receive after traversing difficult times offer us growth, a way to thrive after loss, and a way to bring meaning to our trying times. When we are open to seeing that they are gifts, we can then be open to receiving them. We can let them be part of the alchemy that happens when we trust the process of bringing our feelings to our heart.

Today I consider the gift of holding space for, and walking with, people on their grief journeys as gifts, too. To be able to do this work I have had to fully accept the gifts and blessings of my grief journey. To be sure, I have needed the grace to say "yes" to this work, over and over again. I have had to accept all parts of me, even the parts I wanted to get rid of or hide for most of my life. I found that when I did that—accepted, welcomed and loved all parts of me—that I was liberated. I felt like "me" for the first time in my life. I used to think that when I got rid of a certain behavior, or when I achieved a certain goal then I would be who I wanted to be. I learned through this journey that embracing all parts of me paved the way for me to step into the fullness of my being.

Things to Try:

There are many things that can support you on your journey. Here are a few to consider.

1. Make an altar to honor your loved one. On it you can include meaningful objects or something that represents your journey so far.

2. Create a ritual to acknowledge your initiation as it is now. It can be anything that is meaningful to you. This is something you can repeat whenever it feels meaningful to you.

3. Make a list of all of your blessings. Is there a difference between the blessings you associate with your grief journey and other blessings?

QUESTIONS FOR YOUR JOURNAL:

- Have you noticed synchronicities around important milestone days?

- How do you define blessings and grace? What do they mean to you?

- What would have to change for you to consider that blessing and grace can come from your grief journey?

- What are some of the gifts or blessing you have seen in your life, related or not related to grief or loss?

- It it easier or harder to accept a gift not associated with loss?

- How will you recognize that you have received a gift from a difficult situation?

I was driving to work one morning this week and was struck with
this thought: "Someone else has Leah's heart."
Until this time I had not thought much about
the fact that Leah was an organ donor.

From My Journal, 1/2004

CHAPTER 12

Connections and Touch

One day everything Leah has touched will be gone.

The thought hit me like a thunderbolt. *No, I won't accept that.* The tears
came fast. We were getting ready to move, packing up our house and
moving from Maryland to North Carolina. It had been seven years since
Leah died. We didn't make a rash decision. The time was right—Dan and I
both knew it—and yet, we are moving away from memories we made with
Leah. Was it really true, that someday we would not have anything that she
touched? That the connection we have through the common household
items we all use daily would be gone? I looked at my key ring. On it was
Leah's key ring, the one she used when she died. I will use that as long as I
have keys. Her touch was long gone from the fabric. It's a connection point
for me nonetheless. I don't talk about this; I don't think anyone knows
except Dan. I find myself fingering the woven fabric occasionally, when I
am holding my keys, getting ready to go to the car, or talking to someone.
And I remember they were Leah's, and I wonder if she fingered the fabric
when she was talking to someone, too.

As I looked around the house I saw all of the things she touched that she
would never touch again. I picked up a vase she made in art class. It has a shiny
hard finish and it holds flowers or pencils. It came from her hands. She shaped
the clay; she carved her name and the date in the bottom. I wonder how I will
ever let go of anything she touched, as if the things that she touched would

keep me connected to her. The vase was next to my bed so I saw it first thing when I woke up, and it comforts me.

There's something in the connection of Leah's touch that fascinates me. I was obsessed for a while about the things that she touched, the things that were hers. To this day, I've kept the vase through several moves and it now holds pencil and pens on my desk. Her whole name is on the bottom, not just her initials. Seeing her name scratched in by her hand brings a variety of reactions. Sometimes I can't bear that she is no longer here. Sometimes, seeing it makes me smile. Mostly, I am in wonder that something that she made is still a part of my world. From where I am now, sometimes the connection to her doesn't always feel strong. I look at her vase and I wonder what was she thinking when she made it. What made her pick the glaze colors that she did? Did she make it for herself or for someone else?

So, no, the things she touched would not all be gone. It's more symbolic for me. In preparation for our move, I set aside a few things I want to keep, like her key ring, the vase, her photos, and a sweatshirt, as did Dan and Peter. I also invited some of her friends over to take something of hers to remember her by—something that would help them stay connected. I didn't know how meaningful that was until her friends came over and just asked to sit in her room by themselves.

A Father's Thoughts

Dan told me that he felt like we were invading her room after she died. Her space was filled with memories. There were the objects that she touched, the clothes she wore, and the accumulation of things that collect in the bottom of a drawer or the back of the closet waiting to be sorted through. Coming across a photo, or a notebook page of things she saved, made both of us wonder what she thought about this or that, or what the events were that brought those smiles to the faces of friends in the photos. One thing we had were plenty of pictures. He remembered that she always told us to take plenty of pictures. How precious they are now, and how they can reignite such strong memories.

As we were getting ready to go through her room, Dan recalled, "I remember opening the door to her room looking in and gazing at her things, not being able to step into the room but standing in the doorway looking from object to object."

He saw our young girl's room in a whirlwind of chaos. The clothes left in a heap, an unmade bed, dirty dishes, the paper scraps, knickknacks, books and magazines that would have made him crazy at one time. That day he asked himself, "Why did I ever attempt to get her to clean up her room?"

He thought of the many times he felt that he should just do some of the cleaning himself and avoid the "look"; that roll of the eyes that was meant to pin him in place and make him feel the brunt and ire of her teenage wrath. But as he stood there that day, alone in the doorway and it wasn't with the same attachment or emotional urgency as when he looked at "the mess."

Going through her things was a chore that was not easy to start, and seemed to get more difficult the deeper we went into those mementos. There were buttons from an ice cream shop from a long ago vacation, the box of broken crayons that was a collection from every new school year's requirement list, the "fashion police" button that Dan had given to her for reminding him to be aware of how he looked. The many drawers, boxes and containers were solid reminders of the dreams that would never come true and which contributed to our grief.

Your Own Connections

You may have your own way of staying connected to your loved ones. Again, the connections to each one will be as unique as the relationship you shared. It's not necessary to go through your loved one's room or things until you are ready. Sometimes sitting in a room can bring comfort, and sometimes it is too much to bear. Honor whatever shows up for you, and remember that other members of your family may have a different way to make a connection. If it feels right to you, offer something of theirs to friends or family only after you know it's not something you would like to keep for yourself. Sometimes you know right away what you would like, and often times it takes a while for you to recognize the connection as meaningful.

When it comes time for you to let go of your loved one's things, you will know the time is right. This is a time to ask for help and support for yourself as well as help going through, packing, and taking the things away. A friend who did not personally know your loved one will not be as emotionally attached to what needs to be given away and can help to make this process easier for you. Having someone there to support you or make tea and food can also be helpful. Take some time to ask for what you need at this time.

Letting Go, Again

When it came time for us to go through Leah's room for the final time, I asked a friend to help me, one who did not know Leah. While she was sad about Leah's death, she didn't have the same connection and attachment to her things like I did, or Leah's friends did. I stared at the piles of clothes that I sorted through the night before. I let my friend go through the clothes, and put them in boxes to give away. I was ready, or so I thought. It had been almost seven years—wasn't that enough time? Enough time for what— to mourn a daughter, to know she wasn't coming back? So much of the physical side of losing Leah was still difficult for me. I couldn't wrap my head around the physicality of it all.

As I look around my house now, a house in which Leah never lived, I realize I have more things now that she did not touch, than I do of things that she did. We gave away many things that had been a part of our household from when she was here, too, and many things that we have are new. There is a quality to this that feels elusive, especially when I try to grab onto the concept of being connected to her through her touch.

I wonder how this relates to processing grief. Does having a connection to Leah make it easier for me? Do I feel comforted when I look at her name at the bottom of my pencil holder? Or, maybe the things that are hers provide another opportunity to feel my feelings, and that is another way to process grief when it arises. The feelings that make up grief appear differently every time they come up. And then there are the associative feelings that come up when I remember an activity or event that was connected to the object I am looking at.

I took out my mom's wedding rings recently. I had not thought about her for a while, and holding her rings in my hand, turning them over, and remembering how they looked on her hand, brought back memories of her. If I hadn't had come across her rings, would I have remembered her at that particular moment? Or was I ready to remember another part of our time together, so I was led to look at her rings?

Photographs can hold a similar feeling for me. We have pictures of Leah in various places of our house. Recently I looked at her baby pictures. They all made me smile, but when I had a chance to watch videos of her as a child, I sobbed like I haven't for a long time. Maybe it was seeing her as a live person, talking, singing, and moving.

All of these experiences have shown me nuances of my grief journey that I never expected. Sometimes they take me deeper into feelings that I really can't express, feelings that I always feel in my heart. When that happens I always come away with a new insight about my own grief journey, or about grief in general. Sometimes I remember something about Leah that I hadn't thought of for a long time. Sometimes the feeling itself makes me feel like she is near, and her actual presence is making me think of her. I can't help but wonder if the way I experience my own grief journey, now that I am helping others through theirs, is a result or circumstance of the work I do. Walking with others on their journeys takes me to another level of my own grief, and entering another level of my journey is helping me understand my clients in a deeper way. It feels like if I try to analyze this too deeply, it will take me away from the direct experience of my own journey and my own life.

Associative Memories

One morning I took a cup of coffee in the car with me on the way to work. The cup I took was one that was Leah's. I used to use it everyday to take coffee to work, as a way of feeling her presence, but in the last few years, in an effort to cut down on coffee, I stopped that practice. That morning, however, I smiled as I took the cup that she used for hot chocolate and hot apple cider. Half way to work my glove got caught in the handle as I lifted it to drink. I realized that the handle was about to break, and that is when I lost it. *One more thing that Leah touched is about to be broken.* It always amazes me what will take me back into the raw pain. It doesn't matter what it is, these moments are here for me to feel the pain and loss and reflect on the time that has gone by, and all of the heart-opening experiences I have had along the way. I taped up the cup handle with duct tape when I got to work. Duct tape will hold it together for a little longer, until I am ready to let it go. Duct tape is a little like love. It is there when you need it, and it is strong.

An associative memory brings up a feeling that is connected to a seemingly unconnected event. A broken cup triggered my feelings of missing Leah. These memories can catch us off guard and make us wonder if we are regressing, or even going crazy. Sometimes we are not even aware of the connection; the feeling comes out of the blue, leaving us to wonder why we are feeling this way. If we don't make the connection, we can become worried about what is happening to us. Awareness of associative memories is the first step to recognizing them. Associative memories are further discussed in the chapter about milestones and holidays. It is important to mention it here, too, because connections to our loved ones bring up feelings that appear out of nowhere.

Organ Donation

I had a similarly difficult time with organ donation. Leah was adamant about being an organ donor when she got her driver's license. During her hospital stay the organ donor coordinator approached us about donation. Knowing of her wishes, we listened, although I'm not sure how much we comprehended at the time. It was important to us to honor Leah's wishes, but at that time we were still hoping that our miracle would be that she would return to us. When we knew that Leah wasn't coming back, we talked with her again, and asked more questions before signing the necessary papers to donate Leah's organs. She donated her heart, kidneys, liver, pancreas, and the veins in her legs.

Until the time I had the thought about someone else having her heart, I hadn't thought much about the fact that Leah was an organ donor. I was not yet ready to invest emotionally in this area. After that first thought, I began to have frequent thoughts about organ donation. The Maryland Transplant Resource Center calls donors and their families "heroes." I didn't feel like a hero. In the midst of fresh grief I didn't want Leah's heart or kidney or liver in someone else. I wanted my daughter back, plain and simple. The fact that her spirit no longer inhabited her body made no difference to me. I helped make those body parts, and they were mine, if not Leah's. I railed on like this for quite a while. I could not make peace with the fact that Leah was no longer alive, and her spirit was not in her body, yet her body needed to be kept "alive" in order to harvest the organs. I didn't yet want to accept that organ donation is a huge gift. I just wasn't yet ready, and it seemed like I was the only one who was having those feelings. Everyone else thought that it was such a wonderful thing that we did. I wanted a clear-cut line between her life and death. But, like the mystery I have been living since she's been gone, there is no such clarity.

I sat with these feelings for a very long time before I was ready to contact the recipients of her organs. Before I initiated contact, they were still recipients, not real people. I wasn't ready for them to be real people. And yet I know that if Leah was offered a brain transplant, if that were even possible, I would have scraped and clawed to the end of the earth to get that brain in her head if it would have meant she had even the slimmest chance of living. As I sat with both sides of these feelings, I began to realize that I needed to make contact to offer the recipients, the people that now carried Leah's organs, an opportunity to know her. It has helped me to come to terms with this aspect of losing Leah.

In February of 2004 I mailed the letters to the recipients of her organs, through the Transplant Center. They would contact me if they get responses to my letters. By the time I wrote the letters, I no longer needed answers. I just wanted to let them know a little more about Leah.

A few weeks later, I heard from the Transplant Center that the recipient of one of Leah's kidneys had died. I didn't want to know this. I had lost enough. I grieved for her kidney and for someone I didn't know, and prayed for their family.

In the months that followed, I received a response from the recipient of Leah's liver, as well as from the mother of the girl who received her heart. I wondered what it was like having her heart, if the girl could feel its goodness, its wildness. My own heart remembers every nuance of her from the moment she was conceived. What does her heart remember? So many mixed feelings, so much love.

Organ donation is another part of the mystery. Near the milestone of her death I think of the recipients of her organs, and send them prayers and blessings.

Things To Try:

Here are some suggestions to keep your connections strong.

1. Have a special place in your house for some special items that belonged to your loved one. Or, place meaningful objects around your house as reminders.

2. What are your associative memories? Make a list and continue adding to it as you remember or experience them. Knowledge that a certain time of year reminds you of your loved one can help you be ready when these feelings arise.

3. Ask for support when you need it as you are going through personal items, even if it is not yet time to let them go. Ask for support when it is time to let them go.

QUESTIONS FOR YOUR JOURNAL:

- Do you have something of your loved one that brings you comfort?

- How do you continue the connection with your loved one?

- What does connection mean to you?

- Are there layers to your grief that complicate your grief? Can you unravel them and look at one layer at a time?

- How do you feel when you contemplate letting go of your loved one's personal things? What do you need to go through this process with more ease? You may need to ask yourself this question again and again. Remember you don't need to act until you know you are ready.

"And I'm giving you a longing look
Everyday, everyday
Everyday I write the book"

—Elvis Costello

CHAPTER 13
Everyday Grief

Redefining Grief

As I lived my life up until the time of my daughter's death, I didn't identify a lot of my experiences as grief. Yes, there were daily disappointments, frustrations and setbacks, but on the whole I considered my life to be going well, and getting better. I was even aware that I was learning from those daily disenchantments.

There were moments in my life that I identified as grief. Among them were the death of my grandparents and my first birth experience. However, at the time, the everyday experiences of pain, regret, and frustration passed unnoticed as grief. Yet, these moments became the subtext to the lines inscribed as my story was written. All of the major events in our life—births, graduations, weddings, accidents, divorces, health issues, and deaths—weave our stories. They are major themes, telling of the passage of our existence on this planet. The myriad of seemingly minor incidents that also make up our stories goes unnoticed, and when they do, they accumulate as additional layers in our stressful lives.

Returning to everyday life after Leah's death had a different dimension to it than the life we knew before. Our perspectives were changed. Normal feelings took on new meanings. They were redefined by the events that broke open our lives. For example, before our loss, when we thought about numbness or silence, our experience was probably much more universal, thinking perhaps of the numbness after dental work, or the silence of the early morning at sunrise.

Afterwards, my husband Dan had a more personal understanding of numbness and silence. He speaks of the numbness he felt after the accident and how there was a shift in his view. He knew that grief was there, but he was incapable of describing what the lack of feeling was really like. He remembers his feeling of emptiness when he walked past Leah's bedroom door, knowing that she no longer occupied the room. The music no longer played. He didn't hear her TV playing late at night when we all should have been asleep. It was the silence of loss that he found clamoring in his mind. It was something that was hard to get used to or understand. No laughs or giggles, no whining, nothing. Just silence. And the numbness that wouldn't let him cry or release the pain of loss. It was a layer of grief that he didn't expect.

Our Daily Grief

My realization that grief is a lifelong journey served me well as I came to terms with my own daily struggles. We experience grief in many forms and many different ways. We dismiss our daily disappointments and frustrations as too minor to give our attention to, or we may tell ourselves that we are too busy, or that our griefs are not important and will dissipate on their own. In actuality, they are more likely to accumulate and affect our health through stress, worry, anxiety, and depression. We likely do not even know that we can learn the skill of being with our grief.

How many morning or afternoons have you endured heavy traffic on your way to or from work? At how many railroad crossings have you sat completely still, waiting for the caboose to pass, so you could be on your way? How about the aggravating driver who makes your commute an ordeal by tormenting you with bad driving habits? How many hours have your spent waiting in doctor's waiting rooms, emergency rooms, or dental offices?

What about airports, flight delays, baggage claim waits, long lines at the security checkpoint? Maybe it was the wait for the copy machine at the office, the long line at the grocery store, or the long wait for your turn at the salon, just before a holiday, that caused you stress.

Have you ever been distracted by someone else when you are pursuing a hobby you enjoy for relaxation? In all of these examples, what keeps you in a stressful state instead of being present to your task at hand, or truly enjoying what you are doing?

We may consider these events trivial, but when you can bring awareness to these stressful moments, you can identify ways to diffuse what may feel like an escalating torrent of emotions. When you can recognize these insignificant events as an important part of your story, you can develop skills and resources to diminish your emotions when they feel so swollen they are ready to rupture. The resources you put into practice to process your daily disappointments and smaller heartaches will greatly assist you when bigger occasions of sorrow arrive.

We tend to internalize much of what happens to us during the day as a result of not wanting to inappropriately act out. We marshal our discipline in our attempt to control what we can, and let the rest take care of itself. What if we the skills we learn to ease our daily stresses can also assist us when we come face to face with an unexpected trauma?

How many of us are like the little duck in the pond, truly letting our troubles run down our backs and shaking them off our tails? Our bodies were not made to endure pent-up emotion and stress. What if we could learn to let off steam in a healthy manner when the pressure becomes too much, instead of allowing our emotions and feelings to roil in our gut? Much of this is learned behavior taught to us by our parents, grandparents, teachers and peers.

There was a time when society understood the waxing and waning of life. It applied to sunup and sundown, planting and harvest, birth and death rituals. Much has changed with modern times and the influx of technology. The lessons that were once taught to us have become clouded in the constant messages that we get through the media. These messages are confusing, and when misinterpreted can have tragic results and consequences that can linger for years before we understand their meanings. We have lost sight and have not been prepared to grasp the natural order of picking up, passing on, or setting down the torch. Historians point to when people moved from the farm to the cities as the beginning of our loss of connection to the land and the natural connection to these rhythms. One could argue that our original understanding of being human and mortal has become distorted. We no longer understand the way our food is made. We eat more processed foods and we are less likely to take the time to cook our food, in favor of the expediency of fast food. Could you explain how our energy is delivered, or how our water and sanitary systems operate? In many ways, we have chosen ease over real knowledge.

Many of us who have made that choice believe that if we eat this or drink that, then our world will be wonderful, our fortunes will be secure, and our youths will never fade. The endless line of products to furnish, clothe, transport, sustain, augment, enhance, and beautify our lives cloaks the underlying truth of our humanity, and does not hint at the darker themes that inevitably will surface. They can even serve to distract us from our daily disappointments. In our lifetimes, we will experience the deaths of loved ones. We will grow old. Our bodies will begin to decline. We will experience other life events that cause us to wonder why our lives didn't turn out the way we thought they would. When we lack the resources to confront the anxiety and grief that manifest from these events, our feelings wait underground unattended and can appear unexpectedly when something unforeseen reminds us of our loss. Without the resources, tools, and skills to face our emotions, we suffer.

Myths of Grief

Many of the common ways of dealing with grief are really myths. Some of the most common myths are:

Don't feel bad. Feelings aren't good or bad, they just are. When we are told how to feel, or how to not feel, our feelings are buried underground, where they fester until they show themselves in an inappropriate ways.

Keep busy. Staying busy when we are feeling pain can exhaust us, and certainly distracts us. Our busyness does nothing to help resolve our painful feelings. They go underground and begin to make us feel worse, not better.

It takes time. Time alone does not heal. It's what you do with that time that makes the difference.

Grieve alone. Grieving alone can isolate us and add to our pain. Yes, there are times to be alone along our grief journeys, and there are times we need support.

Be Strong. This myth tells us that to cry or show our pain is a sign of weakness, or a bad example for others; when you are broken, it is nearly impossible to be strong.

These myths are handed down through the generations. We hear the stories not only through our parents and grandparents, but also from teachers, ministers and every other manner of authority, and social media. These voices have a powerful impact on our actions and exemplify the damage we do when we listen to the "quick fix" rather than searching for a method to meet grief that resonates for us.

When something bad happens that we can't change, we admonish ourselves with a list of the "shoulds" and "shouldn'ts" that can impair our self-respect and contribute to many of the destructive behaviors that cause our lives to go off track. These myths are modeled for us in much of our mainstream experience and influence our observational learning. We learn by seeing and by doing. When we take our cues from the way people act and respond to their own grief, we subconsciously assume their behavior, and the pattern continues. Likewise, when we see someone in grief who has turned to a behavior that reduces his stress, we can accept that behavior. However, when the behavior becomes a crutch that negatively impacts his life, we might hesitate to point it out or help him recognize the harm that this may be causing. These types of negative behaviors—like any excessive behavior—can do more harm if left untended.

Grief is the normal feeling associated with loss. When we are told not to feel grief or not to talk about it because it makes others uncomfortable, we stuff away the feelings and bury them so that they are not expressed. When we do this, our grief can't find appropriate outlets and we again suffer. This type of grief is unresolved, and results from being unwilling to face our pain. This applies not only to the loss of a loved one through sickness or death; it has many other expressions. A divorce or the loss of a relationship is an easy example to understand. Holding on to the feeling that this might have been "the one" can cause someone to linger in her feelings and not release the "stuff" that no longer serves them. By not facing what went wrong in a relationship, valuable lessons are left unlearned, or the learning is delayed until another loss comes up, bringing the old feelings with it.

Other examples include the loss of a job, retirement grief, loss of health, moving or relocation, pet loss, or the loss experienced by foster care parents when they have to return a child. More than 40 different types of grief have been identified, and each type brings unique issues to the griever. It is easy to understand that grief is not the same for everyone, and that a single cure can't be applied to some situations.

Dan's Journey to Wholeness

As Dan entered the territory around grief, a lot of baggage came with him. There was unresolved, unshed armor that he carried; not only was there the unspeakable grief of losing his daughter, but also years of unresolved, unspoken turmoil that he had seen on his life's journey. He eventually learned that there was a better way to approach his grief, and that included reaching deep and excavating the accumulation of his everyday sorrows. Dan's search for meaning and healing for long-held grievances began only after he sought help following the devastating loss of his daughter. His first reaction was to compartmentalize, putting away his feelings until he felt he could deal with them. He went back to work soon after the dust had settled, returning to his day job. He believed the myth that if he kept busy, he could push through. With the loss of Leah, his priorities changed, which affected his career. His new priorities influenced the decisions that he made to find help for himself. He admitted to himself that compartmentalizing wasn't working, and that he couldn't do it alone. He was fortunate to find someone to coach him. It was the beginning of his own journey back from the depths of his grief, as well as the investigation of his own inner work, that would lead him to a better understanding of who he was as a man and prompt him to search for a deeper purpose in his life.

It was years later, when I began doing grief work with individuals, that Dan found something that made sense to him and honored his way of processing grief. It was the work of John James and the Grief Recovery Method (GRM) that spoke to him, as a way to help others on their grief journeys. The GRM is based on personal experience, and focuses on the occurrences of grief that occur throughout a person's lifetime. Dan became certified as a Grief Recovery Specialist, and now helps people understand, work with, and begin to recover from their grief in a meaningful way.

The Grief Recovery Method uses a process that assists the griever with communicating and expressing the things keeping him stuck in the loss and grief cycle. In the process, the griever gains understanding of how he can express thoughts and feelings that needed to be different, better, or more than the way he left them after the loss.

Dan's own journey helps him to empathize with the people that he works with; he helps them recover from their sorrow, releasing the pain that they hold and the many daily grief triggers that they experience.

Things To Try:

Here are suggestions to begin to bring awareness to your everyday moments of grief or disappointment.

1. Make a list of all of the disappointment and moments of grief throughout your life. Include events of varying magnitudes, from childhood disappointments to present day losses.

2. Write down all the ways you process everyday stress. Is there anything on your list that helps you meet grief? You can continue to add to your list as you discover new resources.

QUESTIONS FOR YOUR JOURNAL:

- Have unresolved grief issues come up after the loss of a loved one?

- What Myths of Grief have you found yourself falling into without knowing it was a myth? What was your experience?

- What would change for you if you looked at everyday setbacks as having an element of grief in them? How could you use lessons learned about everyday disappointments in your bigger losses?

Christmas was not the same without you, Leah.
Your joyful exuberance was missed.

—From My Journal, 12/29/2000

CHAPTER 14
Holidays and Milestones

Days on the Calendar

We all acknowledge different days when we consider loss. We always know that the day someone dies is a significant day. For parents, a child's birthday is often difficult, and not everyone thinks to acknowledge that. There are many ordinary days that bring to mind our loved ones. Some of them may be unique to you and your family, and the traditions you created together; to most of us, that same date may be just another day on the calendar. To you, the last Friday before school starts may bring up painful memories; it might have been a day you spent with your parent, or child—a day special to only the two of you. Now that they are no longer physically in your life, this day is difficult to you. It can be helpful to make note of the days that hold special places in your heart—the ordinary days, as well as the milestones and holidays that are universally celebrated. Awareness of these times can help you be prepared for the feelings that you may experience. Without this awareness, our feelings may seem to hit us out of the blue… and then we remember why.

Our Changing Traditions

We sat in the living room looking at our undecorated Christmas tree. We sipped coffee, waiting for Peter to get up. He had arrived home from college the previous day. Boxes crowded out our living room. Dan put on some Christmas music. I started crying—Leah was not here to help us decorate this year. It hit me once again. My heart felt as bare as the tree sitting in our window waiting for adornment. How were we supposed to do Christmas without Leah being here? We turned the music off.

When Peter got up, we started the decorating process. He and Dan began to string the lights on the tree. I noticed the stark silence in the room. I noticed there was no music playing, and that the song we usually played and sang with glee while decorating the tree, "Round and Round the Christmas Tree," was pointedly not on. We continued to work in silence; I sorted through the ornaments while the lights continued to be strung. When the lights were done, we each began to dress the tree with ornaments. We saw the special ones that Peter and Leah received each year, marking particular accomplishments. I couldn't bear to see all of Leah's special ornaments going on the tree without her usual commentary. We finished the tree in record time; we didn't turn on the lights as we usually did. Peter returned to his room as soon as we were done. Dan and I put the empty boxes away. We came across our Christmas village, the one Leah took pride in putting up herself. We put that box away without opening it. We both sat on the couch and cried, the unlit tree looming in our view.

What meaning did Christmas have now? How could we do this, year after year, without Leah? This was the second year without Leah in our lives. What did we do the first year? That year we were still numb. It didn't matter what we did. The loss was still fresh. The pain still protected our hearts from feeling fully what it meant to be without Leah's presence at Christmas. This second year was different. We marked the first anniversary of Leah's death on November 8th, and then our second Thanksgiving without her. The dread began to mount in early fall as we remembered preparing for her senior year in high school, shopping for the last time with Leah to buy her homecoming dress, registering for the SAT, filling out college forms. Entering the three-month period that began with the anniversary and ended with the holiday season was excruciating. Even though we had been living without her for almost a year, something about these milestones and holidays magnified the intensity of our feelings. We tried to do that second Christmas like we had always done: the tree, the Christmas village, baking cookies, presents, our meal. It hurt too much. Afterward, when we had a chance to recover a little, we realized that we needed to change the way we celebrated; we could not continue to try to recreate what was no longer there.

The next year we began to travel during the holiday season. This changed several things; we didn't have to decorate because we weren't going to be home. We didn't have to shop for presents because the trip was our gift. We didn't have to bake cookies or cook a big meal. We began to change our traditions and create new ones.

Associative memories play a big part in the way grief appears during the holiday season, too. Our memories are attached to something from a certain time in our past. It can be a food, a smell, a song, or an event—anything that reminds us of the past.

The smell of risotto cooking reminds me of my grandmother. The smell of Christmas trees reminds me of going out in the cold, snowy weather and looking for a tree when I was a child. Seeing a snow village at Christmastime reminds me of Leah. She loved the ceramic town we had and she always arranged it. It is one of our Christmas traditions that we have not been able to resume since she has been gone.

Changing traditions

The holiday season can be stressful on it own, without the added layers of grief. Grief is a difficult emotion to describe because of the many other feelings that can come with it: sadness, anger, devastation, and so many more. During holidays, these feelings often show up in different intensities, at different times, for each member of your family.

What helps you cope one time, may make you dissolve into tears the next. Having some skills, or some alternative traditions to draw on when you find yourself hit by intense feelings, can help you to cope with the holidays. Here are a few that worked for me.

Change the location of your celebration

When we began traveling during the holidays, we still missed Leah, and remembered past holidays. However, we were not faced with everyday reminders that we were not ready to face. The change of scenery took us out of our normal environment and provided another layer of relaxation and stress relief. We often planned vacations to warm tropical locations. Traveling to a new destination can take you out of the familiar that may be too painful for you.

Change the way you decorate

It became too difficult for us to put up a Christmas tree and decorate it with all of Leah's special ornaments. We decided not to put up a tree the after the second year, and we have not put up a tree since. Our decorations have become simpler. One year we got a small potted Christmas tree, and decorated it with homemade ornaments. We often get a poinsettia, an amaryllis, or paperwhites. Make your decorations match how you are feeling, or try something you have always wanted to try, like a homemade wreath or garland instead of a tree.

Christmas music

We stopped listening to Christmas music for a while. There were certain songs that were special to our family that were just too hard to hear in the first few years. We gradually started including music again. Now, in limited amounts, the memories soothe us, although there is nothing that catches me off guard like hearing a song—tears spring up without warning at times.

Shopping

Shopping at the mall was too difficult for Dan the first few years. It was not just the festive atmosphere, but also the memories of shopping trips with Leah. He began shopping online. Shopping with Leah was a common pastime for the two of us. I avoided the stores we frequented for some time, because just walking into one of them was enough to bring on the tears.

Self-care is especially important during times of stress

When I am feeling stress my grief becomes overwhelming. Give yourself some extra self-care during the holiday season. You can keep a list of things that nourish and comfort you. When you are feeling stress or are overwhelmed, take a look at your list. You can choose something from your list without having to think of what you want to do when you are already feeling stress. Some suggestions to get your started are naps, a bath, a walk in nature, or a cup of tea. Make your list meet your own needs. This is a time to be diligent with your self-care rituals. Include extra self-care to help with relaxation. To this day, when I am feeling stressed, my grief is closer to the surface. Become familiar with your own grief triggers and learn what works for you to help ease them.

Grief Changes with the Seasons

What worked this year may not work next year. There is no right or wrong way to meet your grief, and no timetable on when you will begin to heal. Give yourself the time you need, and honor your own process. Each member of your family will process grief in her own way, too. You can let her know that her way is ok; sometimes all that is needed is to know that however we are processing grief, and wherever we are on our grief journey, is exactly right for us. That can be enough to allow us to relax a little, and let the healing begin.

Some years you will feel like your loss happened yesterday. Other years you will receive insights that provide you with a new level of understanding. This will not happen in any particular order. Grief is a changeable journey. Your willingness to be with it as it arises will help you relax and remind you that you are not regressing. Remember, all healing happens in a relaxation response.

Here are some questions to help you decide what is right for you:

- Where would you like to spend time this holiday season?

- Will familiar surroundings comfort you?

- What kind of decorations feels right for you and your family this year? The answer may be different next year.

- Is there holiday music that is too difficult to hear this year?

- Are there times that music can soothe you?

Give yourself permission to sit with these questions in the days leading up to the holiday season. Trust the answers you receive. Remember to be gentle with yourself at this time.

Other Milestones

Milestones such as the anniversary of your loved one's passing, his or her birthday, your birthday, or birthdays of other family members will also be difficult. The same guidelines apply to this type of milestone. Marking the anniversary or a birthday can be bittersweet, but it can bring together friends and family who are also having difficulty, and allow you to support one another. On Leah's birthdays, we often eat some of her favorite foods and raise a glass to her memory. Associative memories play a part in these milestones, too. It is important to be aware of them, because they can surprise you; both with the memories they evoke, and by the intensity of the feelings.

There are other milestones that may catch you off guard, or milestone days that are special to your family. Here are a few of my difficult milestones.

A change in the Season
One year I began to feel a sense of dread, a familiar feeling that arose as the anniversary of Leah's passing drew near. It took me by surprise, especially when I looked at the calendar and noticed it was only the end of August. Then I noticed the weather; that year the cool weather came early. This is a good example of an associative memory. I associated the feelings of the milestone time with the cooler weather that year, rather than with the calendar.

A new school year
The start of a new school year has always been full of nostalgia. Ever since I had children in school, the end of summer and the start of school year have always been bittersweet. The start of a new school year brought to mind how much

growth had occurred for my kids. The anticipation of a new school year, with its new clothes, new school supplies, and the crispness in the air, marked the passage of time in a way that a new calendar year never did. After Leah died, this time of year became especially poignant. For a long time, the associative memories that accompany this time of year were too much to bear.

A new school year meant I was headed into another milestone day—another anniversary of Leah's death, another reminder that she would be forever 17 ½. I wanted to bury my head in the sand at the first cool breeze that came over the mountain and not emerge until after Christmas. Fall, Thanksgiving, and Christmas all conspired to remind me of my pain. This season is rife with associative memories as it is, without the additional layer of missing my daughter.

Birthdays

My 50th birthday coincided with the completion of our house renovation. Part of that renovation was the installation of an arbor in Leah's honor. It is a place outside to sit and meditate, and enjoy the flowers and trees. We dedicated the space on my birthday. I spoke of the process of our renovation and how the outside space became Leah's new room—a place she could visit when she wanted. As I sat in reflection the morning before the dedication, I became aware of her presence and her birthday present to me. She told me that the space represented her spirit as she had become. I had been asking for that insight for such a long time. What a fitting birthday present.

Graduation

As the time for Leah's senior class to graduate approached, I became filled with dread. Graduation is another milestone, one that marks an ending and a beginning. All of her friends would be leaving high school and continuing their lives. Would this be the way they would be able to put this behind them? Was it that easy? The thought of attending a graduation ceremony without Leah being there was too much for me to bear. I didn't know how I could go. I didn't want to go, yet I couldn't stay away.

We had reserved seats, up near the front. I felt everyone staring at us, whispering, "They are so sad." I wondered if I was making others uncomfortable. Was our presence putting a damper on the celebration?

We noticed a lit candle on the stage in front of a picture of Leah. We were in a daze, wondering why we had come. All her friends looked so grown up and so serious; none of them made eye contact, all of us trying to be brave. We watched each student come up to get his or her diploma. I felt proud, and I know Leah did, too. Dr. Paulette Shockey, the principal, gave the following speech:

> *On November 8, 2000, all of us were brought closer to our own mortality by the untimely death of our student, friend, and classmate, Leah Loeffler. The following poem is a tribute to her:*
>
> *There is an old belief that each person is sent into this world*
>
> *With a special message to deliver*
>
> *With a special song to sing for others,*
>
> *With a special act of love to bestow.*
>
> *No one else can speak our message,*
>
> *Or sing our song.*
>
> *Or offer our acts of love.*
>
> *They are entrusted to only one.*
>
> *According to this tradition, the message may be spoken, the song sung, the act of love delivered*
>
> *Only to a few,*
>
> *Or to all the people in a large city,*
>
> *Or even to all the people in the whole world.*
>
> *It all depends on the unique plan for each person.*
>
> *As we remember Leah Loeffler today we want to say*
>
> *Your message has been heard in our hearts*
>
> *Your song has warmed our world,*
>
> *And your love has brightened our darkness.*
>
> *Thank you, Leah, for your message, your song, and your love.*

Her name was announced, and the entire class stood in one motion. We went up to receive her diploma. As I took it and walked offstage, everyone in the class moved their tassel from left to right at the same time. They had waited for Leah to get her diploma to do that. As I walked back to my seat, there was not a dry eye in the auditorium. I knew it was the right decision to come, for both us and for her class.

Weddings

Weddings have been hard for us since Leah died, knowing we would never celebrate her wedding with her, nor witness her stepping into partnership with her beloved. Dan would never walk her down the aisle or dance with her at her wedding. The first several weddings we attended were the most difficult. Seeing the bride escorted down the aisle by her dad was almost more than we could bear. We would step outside for the father- daughter dance at the reception. We did what we needed to do to care for our fragile psyches. As hard as these times were for us, it was important for us to honor each new bride and groom as they made a new family. It was a way for us to affirm life and celebrate with our friends and family.

We emerged from each wedding celebration knowing that our attendance at the party was as healing for us as it was for others who know our story.

As you approach a milestone, ask for support. It is not always easy to ask for help in the best of circumstances. When we are grieving it can be harder. If you would like someone to accompany you to visit your loved one's grave, for example, you can do that. If you want his or her silent support, tell them that. A friend is always grateful to know how they can help. If they have not experienced a significant loss themselves, they may not be sure of the best way to help. Making your needs known helps you and them.

Big Milestones

Somehow, no matter how long I have been on this path, big milestones have always packed a bigger punch. Five, ten, fifteen; for some reason those numbers hold more expectation. They mark time in a different way.

One Year

On the first anniversary of her death we spent the week in Barbados. The tropical breezes soothed our battered emotions. As we sat on our terrace on Nov. 8th, a sparrow flew up. I was sure Leah sent it. We thanked her. There was so much anticipation leading up the one-year anniversary. The most important lesson I learned in the first year was my willingness to stay the course. Each day I made the commitment to be with my feelings, whatever they were. That daily decision was enough at the time.

Five Years

Five years came with much dread and with a sense of the unbelievable. How could that much time have passed since Leah left us? I don't remember how we marked the day; I do remember it was a difficult time.

Ten Years

Time was suspended, speeding up, and nonexistent as we approached the 10th anniversary. Nuances of those times, ten years ago, slid into my consciousness. We were living at the beach at the time, but I was on the way back to Raleigh, heading into the 10th year marker. I met a woman at a rest stop who asked to use my cell phone. She had been visiting her daughter and had left her purse at her daughter's house with all of her money and her cell phone. She told her daughter that in the midst of hugging and saying goodbye, she forgot it. I got back in my car and burst into tears, missing my own daughter.

I thought about the last time I saw Leah, the last time I got a hug from her. I remembered how I felt when I heard she was in the accident. I remembered a feeling I had at the hospital, on the way there, talking to her friends. With each glimpse of the past, I let it be there, knowing it was not really there in that moment. Some of the feelings were not possible to put into words. I felt the desperation of a mother forced to continue on without her daughter. Ten years have passed, and she is still not here.

We both took the week off of work and spent a lot of time in silence and reflection. When we moved to Raleigh, we took the prayer bundles from Leah's Remembrance Gathering with us. We marked the anniversary by hanging the bundles from the Gathering on a tree in our backyard. We had a gentle week, remembering, laughing, and crying. It was the very next year, the 11th, that I willingly entered into the portal of the anniversary, a week or so before the anniversary of her accident, rather than when school started. From this point on, I entered this time willingly rather than with resistance. The change it made in my experience and my healing was exponential.

Fifteen Years

This milestone felt really big to me, and I started off feeling more resistance than I had been feeling for a while on the anniversary of her accident.

> *Resisting feeling makes the suffering greater.*

> *Resisting dams up the grief and it begins to feel overwhelming, like I am going to burst. Resisting going there prolongs the pain.*

> *So I let myself feel the pain.*

> *I let the tears come exactly as they showed up.*

> *I let myself, once again, feel the helplessness of not being able to help my daughter live.*

> *I let myself feel the sadness of missing her.*

Each day for five days I let my grief come in waves. My energy was low all week. I felt sad—sadder than I have in a while. All week long I relived really good memories of Leah, ones that made me smile and laugh. For the first time in a long time I heard songs from her on the radio. I cried. Tears sprang up at surprising intervals, out of nowhere—or so it seemed. Through it all, I could not wrap my head around 15 years.

> *15 years without seeing her light.*
>
> *15 years without touching her.*
>
> *15 years without an eye roll.*
>
> *15 long years.*

On the sixth day, the anniversary of her death, I emerged with new insights. I felt strong. I felt like myself again. My sadness was lifting. This round of the grief spiral provided me with insights into my clients' and perspective clients' hesitancy to enter their own grief journeys, and into the fear that is felt when we enter the unknown. There is the knowledge that if we step onto that path, it will be painful, and it may bring up issues we have not thought about in a long time.

Grief can be like a protective shield around our hearts. If we don't acknowledge it, then we don't have to feel. If we do not feel it, then maybe the grief will all go away. I can tell you that grief does not go away; it gets bigger, stronger, and more overwhelming, and the effort of trying to keep it at bay becomes exhausting.

Yes, I am tired of reliving the accident and remembering that she died five days later. It is nothing compared to the exhaustion and potential health issues that can arise from pushing down or repressing feelings. It takes great courage and heart to feel grief day after day, month after month, year after year. Each time you do, each time I do, the blessings and graces far exceed the pain of resistance.

I am still assimilating this year's gifts, but here is what I know so far:

- I am ready to unconditionally love myself, including all the parts that are difficult to love.

- I am ready to take a stand for myself with myself, and live fully aligned with my Truth.

- I will not sacrifice my self-care, my pleasure, or my desires to fit anyone else's expectations.

- I am willing to be vulnerable.

- It feels vulnerable to state these things here, and you may ask how it this relates to Leah's death.

Her death provided me with a huge initiation, the opportunity to completely deconstruct my life, to excavate my authentic self—the me that I am, the fullest expression of myself.

Grief is not pretty, fun, or cut and dried. It is messy, painful, hard, and real. When you have the courage to enter it—to engage your feelings, to bring them into the light of day—you can get through it, layer by layer, and along the way you may just discover a you that is longing to come out and play.

Things to Try:

Suggestions to help you modify your traditions.

1. When a difficult milestone is approaching, take some time and make space to feel your feelings. You can light a candle, make a cup of tea, sit quietly and invite your feelings into your heart. Are your feelings especially raw right now? Ask yourself what you need during this particular day or time. If your feelings are intense, it may feel right to change your perspective; go somewhere or do something that you did not share with your loved one. You will still miss them, but a new environment can ease the intense feelings.

2. If doing the same thing you always did with them comforts you, then do that. There is no one right answer, and it may change from year to year. Honor yourself where you are, each year a milestone comes around.

3. Take a look at your family traditions. There are many holiday traditions that can bring up painful memories. Take some time with your own traditions and decide what will make you feel less stressed and overwhelmed this year. Are there any that feel too painful? Give yourself permission to do things differently or not at all this year. You may feel differently next year.

QUESTIONS FOR YOUR JOURNAL:

- What holiday traditions are difficult for you?

- How can you modify them to make the holidays easier?

- What are your associative memories? You can make a list for any person you are grieving, or any milestone.

- What milestones are the most difficult for you?

- How can you take care of yourself during holidays and milestone days?

Dan stopped by Leah's accident site and talked to Leah's friends
gathered there after she died. He invited them to our house.
We told them to talk to each other, to be there for each other
and to feel what they were feeling.

—From My Journal, 11/2000

CHAPTER 15
Creating Community

Helping Others Through Grief

You have just heard that a good friend lost a loved one. It may have been in
an unexpected way, or it may have been long anticipated, after a long illness.
Just like there are many ways we experience grief, there are also an unlimited
number of ways that loss appears in your life. When this happens, you may
not know what to do or what to say. You may have anxiety at the thought of
seeing your friend, and consider staying away. It is precisely a time like this
that calls us into action. We are being given an opportunity to step out of our
comfort zones, reach out, and connect with someone on a deep level; we can
offer support to her as she navigates a new loss in her life. We are given an
opportunity to create community, and to model for others a new way of doing
things. When we change the way we respond to a situation, especially one that
has always made us uncomfortable, we begin to stretch our wings. We begin to
grow in new ways.

What if demonstrating how to be with a person who is grieving a loss, helps
others to overcome the fear and discomfort of tending a bereaved friend? What
if, one by one, we change not only the conversation around grief, but also the
framework of our experience of walking our grief journeys? What if we make
it acceptable and normal to minister to the grievers in our midst, the way we
attend to our elders and our children? What if we took care of each other in
ways that make us feel loved, as we learn how to live with the changes that

all losses bring into our lives? This is powerful work that has the capability to dramatically change our lives and the way we live them. I hope that some of the suggestions below will provide you with a starting point to begin to change your own conversation around grief.

We are often unprepared with a ready response when a tragedy occurs and many times we are at a total loss to convey our feelings. How then can we let the person who has experienced loss know that we offer support and compassion through his struggle?

Helpful Things to Say and Do

You can help anyone with any type of grief just by being present and listening, and by giving him support and encouragement. Simply being there for the griever can help him move through his feelings, toward healing. It is important to let mourners feel what they feel at the moment.

Whether you have never experienced grief, or have been carrying your own grief for a time, you can still help others who are grieving. Grieving people need to be able to express themselves and share their grief experience without being judged. They need to know that they have been heard and understood. If you are searching for the right words, here a few suggestions.

When trauma happens, the first thing you may experience is shock and disbelief. Many experience the emotion of sadness. But not long after the trauma comes our human need to try to answer the question, "why?" The reality is that often we can't really know why. A grieving person will likely have heard a lot of theories about why a trauma occurred. Sometimes it's best not to add to the chorus, but to just acknowledge that you don't know.

It's not okay that this happened, or, I don't know why this happened.

Saying you don't know why a tragedy occurs seems so obvious, but sometimes this doesn't get said. In a sudden loss, the pieces don't fit. Sometimes nothing works out right and there is no way to fix it. Saying that you don't know the answers can be helpful because it lets the griever know you won't sugarcoat their grief. Even in a situation such as a divorce, which may have been simmering for a long time, saying the words lets them know that you are a safe person to confide in; it can make their isolation seem bearable. Saying "it's not ok" is giving voice to a griever's wondering about why a loss happened.

It's okay to be angry, and,

I'm a safe person for you to express that anger to, if you need to.

Anger can be an essential part of the grieving process, but we often hesitate to talk about it, because others tend to silence us when we express this feeling. For instance, we may be told, "Oh, don't feel that way," or, "You have no right to be angry at God." By saying you are a safe person to share all feelings with, you help the grieving person know where they can turn. You can create a safe space by not sharing your opinion about what is said, and by not giving advice. Sometimes we just need to be able to say everything we are feeling without fear of another's judgment. A friend who creates a safe space allows us to process our feelings in our own time.

I can't imagine what you are going through, and, I am here to support you in whatever way feels best.

Even if you have faced a similar loss, remember that each loss is different. Saying "I know how you're feeling," can ring untrue. Instead, ask how the grieving person is feeling. And then ask what you can do to help. If they have any ideas about what they need in the moment, do it for them. Remember to respect the boundaries around what they don't want help with. You will be putting some control back into the hands of the grieving person, who may feel like she has lost control, or like she is drowning or floundering without an anchor.

I don't believe God wanted this or willed it.

Finally, if someone says that it is God's will; that God needed another angel; or, that God called them home, remember that a grieving friend or family member is likely hearing these statements from a number of other people. Regardless of a person's beliefs, statements like this are often not helpful, even if some people believe they are true. Affirm the idea that it may very well not be true, and that if hearing these ideas about God is upsetting, that they can ignore those statements and understand that people don't know what to say.

Things to Avoid Saying

Some of the things we say can add pain to the loss that is already felt. Most of the time our intentions are good. We want to help someone feel better, or fix what is wrong. Despite our best intentions, though, we often find ourselves saying or doing some of these things:

Judging the deceased or his or her circumstance.

Think before you speak. Are your words going to be a comfort to the person grieving, or are they going to comfort you?

Everything will be alright, or, Everything happens for a reason.

These statements are not comforting to mourners in pain, and there may not be any way to fix their hurt at the moment. While there may a kernel of truth to these statements, it's likely to take a long time before the truth is discovered by the mourner, and it is a part of a griever's journey to discover what "being alright" means for himself.

It was God's will.

In the greater scheme of things, this is a common belief; however, it is not helpful at the time of the loss. The person you are trying to comfort may be angry at their religion or at God. A griever will need to come to his or her own understanding of God's will.

I am praying for you, when you aren't.

Often this declaration is made at the end of a conversation with the mourner as a way for the comforter to exit to other activities. Stay true to your own beliefs, and your statements will come across as authentic.

At least…

Some of the most discomforting statements made to mourners start with the words, "At least." Steer clear of such statements as:

- At least you have other children.

- At least you can still have other children.

- At least you had (however many) good years of marriage together.

- At least they didn't suffer, or are no longer suffering.

- At least you know they are in a better place.

- At least you're young. You can always remarry.

While these statements are conveyed with good intentions, they are not helpful when a loss is fresh.

Unwelcome advice

We often want to help by fixing what it wrong. This can be a tendency not only when faced with a griever, but in other areas of our life. Here are some things to avoid saying:

- You just need to move on.

- It won't help to dwell on the past (or the death).

- You need to get busy and just forget.

- Aren't you going to go back to work? It will get your mind off the loss.

- I could introduce you to someone nice. I don't want you to be alone.

- Are you able to have another baby?

- Quit throwing your pity party! It's been three months.

- You need to get rid of all of his (her) stuff. (And when you do, can I have the_____?)

- You shouldn't feel that way. (This discounts their feelings and might shut down communication.)

- I know how you feel. (This statement is one quick way to get a rise out of an angry mourner or to shut her down from any further expression of grief emotions.)

- Everything happens for a reason.

- People die every day. It's just part of life.

- It was his (her) time.

- It's all for the best.

- It will get better.

- It will be alright.

When you are with a mourner, be there for him. Listen, and only make statements that let him know you have heard him, that you understand him, and that you love and support him. You may not agree with what he says, and he may be confused or distraught. When you are in an active listening mode, responding with a statement like, "I can see how you might feel that way," you offer the griever acknowledgement without inserting your opinion, judging him, or offering advice. You will become a trusted friend who he may turn to when they are ready to talk more about their process.

An Unexpected Call
Likewise, the calls from friends to ask if we were ok made us feel cared for long after the funeral services were over. They could see that we were struggling, and took the time to ask if there was anything that we needed.

Self-Care—It bears repeating here.

Being gentle and taking time for self-care is another key element in beginning to heal. The emotions that you experience empty your reserves. Not only do you feel that you have cried until you have no more tears, but your emotional capacity will low. When you feel empty, and you or someone else sees you in this state, it is time for practicing self-care. Self-care means different things to everyone; while going to the gym or doing an active sport might help someone, a walk or a cup of tea might be the answer for another. Sitting quietly and just taking things in might be what brings you peace and recharges your battery. Revisit your self-care list to find something that will nourish you where you are at right now.

Social Media

A discussion about social media deserves its place here. Facebook, Instagram, and LinkedIn, to name only a few, have found their places in our daily lives. Many of us start the day by looking at one or more of these platforms. This is the way we celebrate birthdays; see pictures of friends, relatives and their children; and learn about other life-changing events. Social media creates our communities these days. However you view it, it is a great platform for maintaining connection with our friends and family, and also for letting a lot of people know the news at once. With a few keystrokes, you can learn not only about graduations and weddings, but also about illnesses, divorces, and even deaths. When you learn from Facebook that a friend has had a stroke, for example, how do you respond? Do you respond differently on Facebook than you might in person? Remember that when you comment on social media, you are exposing the person who has experienced a loss to comments about *your* comments. Think before you post or comment. Some of the same guidelines mentioned above are applicable here. It might be best to send your friend a private message. Are the protocols different when we are responding to a loss on Facebook, than in a face-to-face encounter? Part of this answer can be generational. Take time to consider to whom you are responding, your relationship with them, and your feelings about social media. Then you can make a decision that is in alignment with your values.

Additional Resources

Food and comfort

One of the things we found very helpful occurred after the dust had settled, our families had returned home, and we attempted to return to work and find a new routine to lives that had been turned upside down. It was the thoughtfulness of neighbors and friends who helped bridge the days until we felt more stable and capable. The gratitude can't be overstated. Not having to cook on those first days back to work—being able to pull a casserole from the refrigerator and heat it up—made caring for ourselves a little easier. It is the little things that make these big transitions bearable, and you appreciate the little touches that convey profound love and caring from another individual.

Busyness or quite time
Our attention and attentiveness is shortened in grief, and focusing on one thing for any length of time is difficult. We can be distracted easily. Fear of being quiet and not being busy can prevent us from sitting still long enough to allow a quiet mind to emerge, or for grace to enter. Encourage the discipline of setting aside time to quiet the mind; exclude these outside conditions, and allow yourself to hear your internal thoughts. We have more to consider than the chatty little voice inside our head. When we are open to our thoughts, they can challenge us; the response we receive may surprise and delight us.

Meditation
We have been asked if meditation conflicts with a person's religious practice. To answer that question, you need to enter a conversation with yourself about the nature of prayer. Meditation can be considered another form of prayer, and a way to receive grace. Growing up Catholic, the idea of meditation seemed alien to me. We were told that prayer was a conversation with God, and that it was a relatively simple way of asking and thanking our Creator. What we were told of meditation—when it was explained at all— was that it was a technique for eliminating distractions, allowing you to clear your mind and allow God to be present. How different this is from a conversation. It is a way of entering our own internal church by setting aside those voices and creating a quiet climate that is available to us, always.

What is different about any meditative practice is approaching it without thinking of the result. To request a prayer to be answered, or expressing gratitude for the gifts and blessings we receive, is one way—call it "intentional prayer." While in meditation you are opening, being aware, and listening for the answers. Think of it as the other half of the conversation. We ask or state our intention; but, to converse, we must also actively listen and allow the answer to be received.

It takes awareness and practice to enter the quiet state within. In stillness you can find an open invitation to explore the rich interior portrait of your soul. The path to this restful interior oasis is like a walk with the person who you are meant to become in this life.

Each life must tread its own path, and discover the bridge between the outer world and the inner.

Being willing to answer your heart's call to a deeper life begins a journey. Healing from loss, grieving, seeking meaning, and finding a way to move on all begin with acknowledging and facing the call to become aware of the possibility that answers are waiting to be discovered. We have the ability to have our prayers answered and the strength to make this journey into wholeness.

Things To Try:

Some ways to assist others who are grieving.

1. Make a list of things to say to someone who is grieving. Look at it when you are called to visit someone who has lost a loved one.

2. Make a list of things that are not helpful to say to a griever. Look at it as often as necessary.

3. If a neighbor or co-worker has experienced a loss, organize others to bring food for a period of 2-3 weeks. A casserole taken out of the freezer and heated for dinner is welcome when a griever is adjusting to a new reality.

4. Offer to do small chores; organize neighbors, friends, or co-workers to do the same. Things like grocery shopping, raking leaves, shoveling snow, or picking up a child from school are often things that seem insurmountable to someone after a loss.

5. Look at social media for examples of how loss is discussed. What resonates with you about what you see? What doesn't? Start a discussion with friends about social media protocols.

6. Have the courage to discuss difficult topics with neighbors and friends. Having a conversation about difficult things before you need to, can help everyone feel more comfortable when a loss or tragedy occurs.

QUESTIONS FOR YOUR JOURNAL:

- When you experienced a loss, what were the most helpful things someone said to you? The least helpful?

- What things that others did for you were most helpful? Why?

- How do you view learning about a loss on social media? Taking time to consider this now, before you need it, can be illuminating.

Leah's Poem

THIS IS THE POEM WE WROTE ON THE DAY OF LEAH'S REMEMBRANCE GATHERING

Leah will always be in our hearts

Your smile is always there to cheer me up.

Thank you for being a Big Sister to my child.

You are beautiful inside and out,

You were an angel on earth, and now in heaven.

I loved it when we laughed about nothing,

I loved every minute I spent with you

and without your joy I could not do,

or become the person I was meant to be.

I wish we could eat a hot fudge brown sundae,

And dance like we used to.

I remember your morning hugs.

I think of how much we have lost,

But also how much we gained having you in our lives

For even the briefest time.

The beauty of your spirit is always surrounding us.

Your spirit is so strong, and is still around us

Your smile will always be strong in our minds.

Your heart will live within us forever and ever

Your smile, laugh will always be with me,

I miss you so much.

Her smile was beautiful,

She shared it with us all.

She lit up every room.

When someone was down, she made you smile.

She left us in the happiest point in her life.

She taught me what it means to love.

Leah taught me how to smile and never stop,

No matter what was on your mind.

Again, Leah made me laugh so hard my stomach hurt,

And always acted so concerned when I told her things.

Every time I saw Leah she had a smile on her face,

She was beautiful!

Every time I think of Leah and every thing she did,

The feelings I have are unexplainable.

How can you describe someone as big as she?

and, if you could, why would you limit it to just words?

There are so many ways to describe what you were to me.

Like a warm summer breeze, you warm my heart.

Your smile and laughter is a form of art.

Your energy and love for danger will stay in my heart,

and the hearts of all of us will be your home on earth.

Earth is merely a step in the journey to heaven,

Lovely Leah, lift our spirits, please.

Blossom, sunrise, hello, the beauty of beginning

Bless this wonderful day, Happy Birthday.

Leah, you are forever like the sunshine making a sparkling day,

You are like the stars that will forever shine.

If words could describe you and your beauty

my heart would have nothing to do.

I loved it when we danced, and when we sang,

I just wish we could have five more minutes

to forget how we were listening to elevator music.

A TIP FROM LEAH:

FOLLOW YOUR FINGERS, YOUR FINGERS LEAD THE WAY.

—Leah's Remembrance Gathering, 4/28/2001

When Leah was about 5, she took ballet classes. Of course she wore a leotard. One day, while I was getting ready to go to an exercise class, she asked me, in all seriousness, if I was going to wear my Nancy-tard.

—Leah, 1988

Afterword

Saving Turtles

One day Leah came into the house after driving home from her friend's house. It was raining like crazy. She and her friend were dripping wet and laughing hysterically. It seemed that on the way home, they came upon a turtle in the middle of the road. They stopped, and tried to coax the turtle to the other side of the road, but it would not budge. Leah picked it up and brought it safely to the other side of the road. She got sopping wet saving the turtle.

Lessons from My Daughter

After writing the words on the pages here, it only seems fitting to tangibly show what I learned from the wild, tenacious, miraculous, spirited child that was my daughter.

The lessons I learned started the moment we gazed into each other's eyes moments after birth and continue today. The experience of being Leah's mother challenged me to be a better person, to look at situations in a different way. She was not a textbook child. She had her own way of looking at the world and it was miles away from my own view. I had to dig deep, ask big questions and trust my self more than I ever had before. She awakened my fierce nature and taught me how to ask difficult questions. Learning how to be the best mother I could be for her broke me open again and again. I had to honor who she was and find ways to meet her tenacious spirit without breaking it. She taught me how to excavate my own tenacious spirit and embrace a part of me that for so long I wanted to hide. She taught me how to find my voice so I could stand up for her, for Peter, for myself. She was devoted to who she was, no matter what anyone else said about her and she taught me to do the same. These lessons were not easy and gentle. At times they were tumultuous and raucous. In our struggles together my intention was always to meet her where she was, and at the same time, before I understood each of our roles, I wanted her to come to my way of seeing things. Her steadfast commitment to her own nature compelled me to go deeper into my own inner work so that I could learn what it meant to mother an independent strong-willed daughter, and later learn how to continue living the legacy she left for me after she died.

This story sums up one of her greatest lessons to me that started out as a lesson for her. It also illustrates my creativity as I attempted to provide my daughter with a new way to look at her life.

More Than one Way to get to the Park

When Leah was a child, she often did things her own way. When she was reprimanded in school, or compared to others, I didn't want that to be a damaging experience for her, I wanted to show her that everyone's experience is valid. She loved to go to the park near our house. The fastest way was a straight shot down 145th street. One day on our way there I took a different route. We started out in the opposite direction and went up and down streets on our way there. Leah kept asking me where we were going, I said, "To the Park" She said, "This is not the way" I said, "Let's see what happens." We continued on our way, and soon we arrived at the park. She looked at me with excitement and ran to play. The next few times we went to the park, I took a different route each time. Sometimes it took longer, and we saw things we may not have seen going another way.

The next time she complained that she was not doing things the way other people were, I told her that just like there is more than one way to get to the park, there was more than one way to learn math, or spelling or even get dressed. Then we'd searched for a way that worked for her. That seemed to calm her fears that she was different than other people. She eventually learned to embrace her differences, and I am thankful that I was able to help her do so in such a simple way.

I continue to use this lesson myself. Whenever I question my path, I always remind myself, there is more than one way to get to the park, and our own path is valid for us.

When you are questioning your own path, I offer you this advice:

There's more than one way to get to the park.

Biography

Nancy Loeffler is the founder of Being With Grief. As a mother who lost her 17-year-old daughter Leah in a car accident in November of 2000, she fully understands the territory of grief. Her daughter's death provided a doorway to her transformation that she never expected. It broke open her heart and showed her a way to break free from limiting beliefs about what was possible in her life. She walks with her clients on their own grief journeys so they, too, can find meaning, purpose, and even joy again after a devastating loss. She speaks often about her journey and is passionate about changing the conversation around grief. She embodies her message and is often found sitting in Samyama, walking in nature, collaging, or taking a dance break.

Nancy Loeffler

www.beingwithgrief.com

CPSIA information can be obtained
at www.ICGtesting.com
Printed in the USA
LVOW12s0319270617
539400LV00002B/363/P